The Role of the Servant

--- Warren W. Slabaugh

BRETHREN PUBLISHING HOUSE
Elgin, Illinois

Printed in the United States of America

Contents

Foreword

The Christian church has always been hard pressed to understand and explain her Lord. And no marvel! If he is indeed God Incarnate, human knowledge must always fall short of perfect understanding. And it was to be expected that the church would resort to analogies in an attempt to relieve, in part at least, the mystery which pertains to this unique person. The most familiar of these analogies are those of the trinity of prophet, priest, and king. He was indeed a prophet, more than a prophet, out of class with John the Baptist, for he revealed God to man in a measure that was beyond the power of any ordinary man, however great. "No one has ever seen God; the only Son, who is in the bosom of the Father, he has made him known" (John 1:18). The central theme of the epistle to the Hebrews is Christ, the heavenly High Priest who entered into the perfect sanctuary in heaven with a perfect offering, once for all, obtaining a perfect salvation. Jesus used the figure once when he declared that "the Son of man came not to be served but to serve, and to give his life as a ransom for many" (Matthew 20:28).

Perhaps the most familiar and popular analogy is that of king. This was in keeping with the Jewish expectation of the coming Messiah, who would sit on the throne of David. The coming deliverer was to be the Son of David, leading victorious armies who would destroy the Gentile enemies and ruling over the Jews in a glorified kingdom. It is significant that Jesus used the term only once (Mark 12:35), and then in a sense of implied disapproval. Certainly, the popular idea that the Messiah would set up a political kingdom was repugnant to Jesus. Gaining his ends by political and military means was decisively rejected by him, not only in the desert temptation but repeatedly afterward. His kingship is real but it is not of the pattern of this world.

But there was another conception of his ministry, even closer to the mind of Jesus. It was by no means as popular as that of king or priest; in fact, to the Jews of his day it was utterly unacceptable. It had its source in prophetic vision, particularly in the new covenant of Jeremiah and the Servant songs of Isaiah. For these prophets the coming Kingdom was not political but individual and spiritual. Israel, particularly the righteous remnant, was not to rule politically, but to assume the role of servant, that through humility and service and innocent suffering she might fulfill her role as the covenant people and so bring redemption to the nations. This strange idea was for centuries not regarded by the Jews as Messianic. When Jesus came he found his people obsessed with a spirit of nationalism which demanded that the Jew rule the world.

But Jesus with an unerring instinct set aside these false ambitions; he found in the role of the Servant the pattern of the Kingdom and of its Messiah. Here is found the secret of his humiliation which found its climax in the cross.

—Warren W. Slabaugh

January 1954

CHAPTER ONE

The Humble Background of the Servant

He had no form or comeliness that we should look at him, and no beauty that we should desire him (Isaiah 53: 2).

We can never fully understand the mystery of the Incarnation, of how God in the process of his revelation to men went beyond the human agents he had used and by a supreme miracle clothed himself with humanity. "And the Word became flesh and dwelt among us, full of grace and truth . . ." (John 1:14). The marvel is not in the outward incidents surrounding the birth of Jesus the Nazarene, but in the fact that this person, though fully human, was also divine, and transcended the human in his moral and spiritual powers. Here was one who could be described only as *unique*—in his moral attainments, in his instinct for truth which enabled him to arrive at a perfect knowledge of the will of God, in the dynamic which enabled him to live as the Son of God, and in the authority to present himself as the Anointed One administering God's redemptive plan for the world. In the John gospel Jesus says, "For as the Father has life in himself, so he has granted the Son also to have life in himself . . ." (5:26); or, in the words of Matthew 11:28, "Come to me, all who labor and are heavy laden, and I will give you rest." And yet we must believe that this uniqueness lay alone in the

---

Note: All Scripture references are taken from the Revised Standard Version of the Bible. Copyrighted 1946 and 1952.

realm of the moral and spiritual; his physical constitution differed not at all from that of all mankind. The gospel records are not concerned about metaphysical differences; that remained for later theologians to discuss.

But this great fact which the John gospel calls the Incarnation, and which Paul describes as a humiliation—"but emptied himself, taking the form of a servant, being born in the likeness of men" (Philippians 2:7)—becomes the more significant in that the earthly life of our Lord was not one of high honor, of riches, of political authority, or of military might, nor even of high intellectual standing among the people of the world to whom he was to present himself as their Savior. His condition was to be that of the most humble, a station which is expressed by a term which stands at the opposite pole from authority and power and all that human opinion regards as most to be desired; he was to assume the role of the Servant. That the Christ should be a servant was not by the arbitrary fiat of God; it was entirely in keeping with the character and purpose of God; this was the highest and perfect way, the only way, by which he would redeem men.

It is not strange then that Jesus' physical constitution and social background should be in keeping with the pattern of the Servant. He was first of all a Jew. The Jewish Scriptures and traditions honor the Hebrew people as the covenant people of God. But viewed in the light of world opinion, both of the first century and of the twentieth, the Jews have not been honored but have been the most persecuted and the least understood and appreciated of all peoples.

The Jews constituted but a small group in the Roman Empire, and they certainly were not highly esteemed. A considerable number of them were scattered throughout the empire; they were the Jews of the Diaspora or Dispersion. The Jews of the land, those who lived in what we call Palestine, had been a political unit under Herod the Great.

At his death Herod's kingdom had been divided among three of his sons. There were richer and more desirable provinces which governors might aspire to rule. Good governors found it a thankless task; evil governors found the spoils of office scarcely worth the headaches of putting down incipient revolts and keeping the peace. The land was poor in natural resources; the soil was rocky; the terrain was for the most part steep slopes subject to erosion unless carefully terraced; the rainfall was that of a semi-arid region, and there were no great rivers like the Nile or the Euphrates to furnish water for irrigation. Added to this lack of natural resources, the heavy load of taxes laid on by both governor and priest helped keep the people living in squalor and poverty.

The Jews belonged to the Semitic world but had been thrust into the world of the West through the process of Hellenization which began with Alexander the Great, and through the political domination of the world by Rome. To the Graeco-Roman world of this period, the Jew was regarded as being in opposition to all men (1 Thessalonians 2:15).

Jesus was a Jew; the Christian church in its anti-Semitism sometimes tries to forget this fact. He shared whatever of derogation the name carried. He could not have been a Roman citizen. Very few Jews attained to that privilege; it was in some fortuitous fashion that citizenship had come to the family of Saul of Tarsus. The social standing of Jesus' family was humble; they belonged to the peasant class. They were not mendicant, depending on alms, it is true; a parasite cannot rate as a servant. They made a frugal living through hard and ill-paid toil and severe economy. Joseph was an artisan, a worker in wood (Matthew 13:55), and Jesus himself followed the same trade (Mark 6:3).

The circumstances of his birth agree with the pattern of lowliness. Bethlehem was an obscure village lying a few miles south of Jerusalem. It might have been prosperous in the ancient times when it became the scene of the Ruth idyll, and probably from its harvests of grain and the vine deserved its name, House of Bread. It had been the home of the great-grandson of Ruth—David, the shepherd boy who became the warrior king of the Hebrew nation. But now it had sunk into insignificance. The Magi expected to find the newborn king in the capital city; to their surprise they were directed away from Jerusalem to a village. The prophet Micah, who was one of the first to speak of a coming Messiah, had pointed out the incongruity of Bethlehem becoming his birthplace.

"But you, O Bethlehem Ephrathah,
who are little to be among the clans of Judah . . ."
(5:2).

And the town of Nazareth, where Jesus grew up, was an obscure place, noted neither for its wealth nor its culture, but rather for the ill-nature of some of its inhabitants.

The infancy section of the Luke gospel tells of the necessity of a long journey from Nazareth to a faraway village to register in compliance with an imperial command, in spite of the hardship which such a journey would impose on the expectant mother. It tells of their being refused lodging at the inn because better-paying guests had first claim upon its accommodations; of the necessity to bed down with the animals in the cave stable. Here Mary's son was born.

Luke tells the story with rare insight and beauty. There is no hint of pity that his Lord should suffer such humiliation. The great honor and worth which were to be his did not demand special privileges; rather, it was fitting that he who was to carry the burdens of men should share their common lot. Had the innkeeper known and given him the best, it would have spoiled the story. It was to shepherds, rough men of the hills, that the angel message came. They who came to the stable that night were of the servant class. The offering which Joseph and Mary brought to the temple was the offering of the poor; too poor to purchase a lamb, they could bring only a pair of birds, as the Law provided. Further, the birth of him who was to be sinless demanded a sin offering for the purification of his mother. No one marked them as they came into the temple that day, this country man with his young wife and babe. An under-priest received their gift and in careless fashion performed the rite of cleansing. They were lost in the throng which poured in and out of the temple.

The rich and powerful alone received special attention from the all-powerful priestly family. It was only the aged Simeon who, unwittingly but under the urge of the Spirit, came into the temple at that moment and singled them out. He was one of the pious souls who longed for the coming of the Kingdom, for that day when the fullness of God's blessings should fall upon Israel. He had prayed for the day of all days and his prayers had been answered with the assurance that he would live to see that day dawn. Suddenly the light broke through the darkness of a hope long deferred; in the babe in Mary's arms he saw the fulfillment of God's promises. Here was the Promised One! The story is one of rare beauty—God honoring the faith of this old saint, his outburst of joy and praise, his words to Joseph and Mary—a scene reminiscent of the ancient patriarchs. But to those who looked on, he was only an old man, a bit in his dotage and much too talkative. The priests, absorbed in their daily duties, saw nothing different from other occasions: the same dreary routine of oft-repeated tasks, the same tiresome, jostling crowds, the noisy babel of voices. Had the high priest been present, he would have caught no vision; the crowds spelled only profits to him and his clique. He was satisfied with the status quo and was not inclined to welcome any Messiah. The vision of angels had been reserved for rude shepherds, rather than for the religious leaders of the nation. Thirty years later the high priest, Caiaphas, had no thought but of annoyance at the Galilean who defended his Father's house against its profanation by the priests.

And so it has ever been; theophanies and revelations

come not to the proud and haughty, though they may have the reputation of being religious, but to some humble saint, so humble as almost to escape notice. If God would give any advance notice of the coming of his Servant, it would be to shepherds rather than to kings, to humble laymen rather than to priests.

In their own city, Nazareth, the even tenor of their life flowed on—quiet, God-fearing people, that they were. If any report of the strange events which had transpired in Judea came to the ears of their neighbors, it would be quickly discredited. Their neighbors would be more likely to remember other phases of the story which would give grounds for slanderous speculations. But they were submerged in the currents of life in Nazareth; it was simply Joseph the carpenter, and his young wife Mary and their child named Jesus, and in time other children, both sons and daughters.

These were the incidents surrounding the coming of our Lord in the flesh. They were marked by their utter humbleness, by their lack of those things which are regarded as befitting the noble and royal. It was a strange contradiction that the Incarnate One should be lowly, that the Magi should find the newborn king of the Jews not in a palace but in the humble dwelling of a peasant. But if we can view the whole scene as God would view it, there dawns on our consciousness an awareness of its fitness. God, who chose to reveal himself in the flesh and through that revelation to save lost humanity, decreed that the Incarnate One should be fully identified with men, not on the artificial level of the proud and noble but fully sharing the vicissitudes and woes of mankind. "Therefore he had to be made like his brethren in every respect . . ." (Hebrews 2:17). The humbleness of his background and of his birth is in keeping with the role he was to play when he opened his ministry, that of the Servant of the Lord. The Incarnation was the supreme miracle of the ages, but the role of the Servant was the supreme paradox. But only in the mind of men, not of God. The whole transaction, the humiliation of him who took on himself the form of a slave in that he was found in likeness as a man, was the rational will of God. For the preaching of the cross, which is symbolic of the gospel, is to them who are perishing foolishness. But it pleased God through the foolishness of the thing preached to save them who are able by faith to see the grace of God. For the foolishness of God is wiser than men, and the weakness of God is stronger than men.

CHAPTER TWO

The Hidden Years

And Jesus increased in wisdom and in stature, and in favor with God and man (Luke 2:52).

We do not possess a biography of Jesus' life. Even of that period which we call the public ministry, the gospels give us a very incomplete account. Of the period before, to the time he was thirty years of age, Mark and John make no direct mention. Matthew and Luke have the so-called infancy stories, each using two chapters. These stories have to do with the birth of Jesus particularly, the central theme being the virgin birth. Luke adds one story of Jesus' boyhood, that of his visit to the temple at the age of twelve. The gospels are not biographies. While the interest of the writers was in part historical, their main interest was interpretation and doctrine. The lack of outline and the miscellaneous character of the material are due in part to the process of transmission. Gospel material which found its place in the gospels had been carried down by oral tradition and consisted of many small units of narrative or teaching; these are called pericopes.

Though surely the gospel records are incomplete (at least one writer told but a small part of what he knew), we may be satisfied that they give us an adequate picture of Jesus' life and thought upon which to rest our faith in him as Savior. We agree that the events of his public ministry are of more importance than the years before, but the interest of Christians has also turned to the hidden years in an attempt to visualize the life of our Lord as a private individual in Nazareth. The apocryphal gospels, which arose from the second century on, attempted to supply part of this need of information, giving particular attention to the infancy and boyhood of Jesus. They are clearly pious fiction, with perhaps some fragment of fact as a background, and were written either to honor Christ or to forward the claims of some heretical movement. They form a rather precarious source of knowledge of the hidden years and must be put to critical tests. They are to be rejected insofar as they contradict the clear-cut pattern of Jesus' life which we know; in their morbid interest in the miraculous, the more absurd the better.

Our main sources of information are: first, the infancy stories of Matthew and Luke; second, our knowledge of the social, religious, and political conditions of the times; and third, any light thrown back upon the years by references in the record of the ministry.

The humble social and economic status of the family of Jesus has already been noted. As to religious status, they did not belong to that select group, the Pharisees, who prided themselves on their loyalty to the Torah and the traditions and on their freedom from defiling contacts. They belonged rather to that large group called the "poor" who, though neither able nor inclined to meticulous observance of the Torah, were religious in a healthy and devoted fashion.

The Jewish child's education began in the home.

Here he learned to recite the Shema (so named from the Hebrew word *shema,* "to hear"—see Deuteronomy 6:4) and other portions of the sacred writings. The synagogue contributed to religious instruction not only in the formal Sabbath services, but in the elementary schools set up for the instruction of boys. Then there were the yearly festivals which were held in Jerusalem and which afforded opportunity to visit the temple and take part in the religious feasts.

The home life of the Jewish people was of high order. Though the daily toil was arduous and the manner of living exceedingly simple, there was a richness in the close attachment between parents and children, there were high standards of behavior, and there was a devotion to God and to the nation. There was little opportunity for higher learning for the poor. And it is evident that Jesus did not receive a professional training in one of the great schools at Jerusalem. On one occasion the Pharisees marveled at his ability to teach, knowing that he was not a scribe (John 7:15). The story of him at the age of twelve indicates that he had an interest in religious matters beyond that of his fellows, much to the surprise of the great teachers.

But we must believe that the home and synagogue training, ideal though it was, was not sufficient to account for the perfection of character which emerged on the pages of the gospels after this period of silence. Others had the same cultural opportunities and were devoted and open to the truth. From a human standpoint, Jesus was the best product of his social and religious environment. This is part of the explanation of his behavior in the temple at the age of twelve. Many Jewish lads early betrayed a healthy interest in religious matters. Perhaps this was the occasion of Jesus' formal induction into the Jewish church. The Jewish boy at adolescence became a son of the commandment, taking upon himself the obligation to keep the Law.

The solemn significance of this step would accentuate Jesus' interest and devotion. But Jesus was more than the product of social and religious evolution; there was an added plus. This cannot be separated by the process of dissection; his humanity was in inseparable union with his divine nature. Christ's was a real humanity, subject to temptation. The secret lies in the mystery of the Incarnation. Already when he was only twelve this was in evidence. He was in the role of a learner, availing himself of the large advantages of Jerusalem. But it is more than a spectacle of the precocious, of a human prodigy. That perfect comprehension of truth and the moral perfection of his character which carried him forever beyond his fellows and put him in a class by himself were already in evidence. These characteristics lay not in physical or intellectual superiority, nor in rank, but in moral and spiritual powers which his humanity could not fully hide.

We may glimpse a picture of him in the home and in the community of Nazareth. In the family there was harmony and fellowship; yet perhaps there were already signs of the cleavage which must always be manifest between the sinful and the sinless. He must have exhibited that higher loyalty to God in which spiritual ties and obligations transcend the human. There must have been something about Jesus—elusive, yet real—seen as early at least as the incident in the temple, which indicated that he was unique, that he was apart from his fellows, even from his family, though he was so fully a part of humanity.

He was independent of his parents, yet subject to them. Though the church has highly honored Mary and even idolized her to the point of worship, though the story of the annunciation in the Luke gospel makes her the recipient of a special revelation from the archangel, still in the days of Jesus' ministry Mary disappoints us. Though she "kept all these things in her heart" (Luke 2:51), she seems to have become strangely forgetful. She and the brothers of Jesus stand apart from the mission which Jesus established. On one occasion they went out to seize him because he was beside himself (Mark 3:21). Other women joined the movement early; Mary does not seem to have been associated with it until the time of his death.

This may indicate that even in the earlier years Jesus was different, yet the difference was so subtle that it was difficult to point out specifically. He was no less industrious; he carried his full share of the common load of the family enterprise. But he was more gentle and considerate. His religious experience was on a higher plane. There was an awareness of God's presence which made him a mystic beyond all mystics. His religious instincts were reaching out to sense the will of God, and his moral perfection early became evident. This was probably not fully apparent to his fellows; to them the difference would be regarded as queerness.

He was a deep student of the Scriptures, not according to the scribal pattern of formulating statutes to be kept or according to the intricacies of the allegorical, but rather finding in them not merely the history of his people, but more—the story of God's expanding revelation to a covenant people, and through them to all men. Underneath the letter he found the spirit; underneath the spatial and the national he found the universal; underneath the temporal, the eternal.

Those sections of the Scriptures which encouraged the nationalistic ambitions of the Jews he discarded, finding the real message and climax in the universal messages of the prophets. He lived in the hotbed of the Zealot movement, and all during his youth he was exposed to its urgent appeals. While he was yet a boy there had been a violent outbreak which demanded the intervention of Rome, and in the process of which the neighboring city of Sepphoris was destroyed with terrible cruelty and loss of lives. Many times, no doubt, the word was passed through the shops at Nazareth of an important meeting to be held at night out in the hills, where rebellion against Rome was being plotted. But Jesus would have nothing of this; hatred and violence were contrary to his nature; they did not fit into the redemptive purpose of God. To his fellows he must have seemed lacking in patriotism. God did not hate the Gentiles; even enemies were to be loved, not as a gesture but according to the principles of right.

Jesus would spend long hours under the stars, in contemplation and meditation. He loved nature, and out on the hillside at sunrise he found himself close to God.

These years were not wasted years. Though he waited a long time to begin a ministry which seemed to be tragically short, no one can say that the waiting was too long or the ministry too short. Faulty human judgment would change everything according to its own notion, but Jesus walked in the knowledge of the will of God. The perfection of his ministry rests back in part upon the quiet processes which went on in his life during the hidden years.

Lew Wallace in his famous book, *Ben Hur,* tells how when the noble Jewish lad Ben Hur was being dragged away to the galleys, at the well of Nazareth a kindly-faced youth brought a cup of cold water to the fainting prisoner. A recent attempt to write a chapter of these years has been made by Ralph Byers in his book, *Munition Maker of Galilee.* The familiar words of Jesus, "My yoke is easy," are the theme of the book. Jesus the carpenter refused to make spears and repair chariots for Roman gold, or even for the patriotic Zealots, and so passed up the easy profits of war work which are held in our generation to be highly respectable and patriotic. The carpenter continued to make yokes and gates and looms, those homely instruments of peace. The trees which the Father had planted were intended for men's good, not their destruction, instruments for tilling the soil, roofs to keep out the rain and cold, never instruments of death. And further, it was the philosophy of the carpenter that goads were unnecessary if the yokes were light and properly fitted to the shoulders of the oxen.

We may never know all the details of those quiet years at Nazareth—and we need not. But we may be assured that what he was when he stepped upon the pages of history in the gospel records gives us a clue to what he was before. Though he was living the life of a private individual, his character was being molded and his vision of God and his Kingdom was becoming clear. Already there were the marks of that uniqueness which he later exhibited; so we need not wonder that he was not fully understood and appreciated. The veil that lies upon the heart of all men has prevented even the best of men from fully knowing him who was the Incarnation of God.

CHAPTER THREE

The Prophet of the Servant

"What then did you go out to see? A prophet? Yes, I tell you, and more than a prophet" (Luke 7:26).

John, the son of Zechariah the priest and Elizabeth, was a prophet. He received the title, *the Baptist* (three times, *the baptizer*—Mark 1:4; 6:14, 24), probably because he insisted that all Jews receive the washing of purification as a symbol of their readiness to enter the coming Kingdom of God. However, John was noted not for the dispensing of a rite but for the prophetic role which he assumed. It was a commonly accepted belief among the Jews that the day of prophecy had long since passed. The great Hebrew prophets who arose early in the Hebrew monarchy and continued until after the exile had made a contribution to the culture of their people second only to that of the lawgiver, Moses. But the period of prophecy had passed. In the canonization of the Hebrew Scriptures, which began after the return from exile, one of the tests of a book was prophetic authorship; no book which arose after the decline of prophecy could find acceptance as Scripture. Many late books were included in the Septuagint, the Greek Bible of the Dispersion, but the Palestinian canon held strictly to the rule that no late book could be considered.

John's appearance on the stage of history was sudden

and dramatic. The strange circumstances surrounding his birth, told so strikingly in the first chapter of the Luke gospel, were known only to those who lived in his near vicinity. He had lived in the desert "till the day of his manifestation to Israel" (Luke 1:80). When finally "the word of God came to John" (Luke 3:2) and he came into the region of the Jordan River preaching the near approach of the Kingdom of God, he came as one unknown. The report went out that a strange man of the desert was preaching at the fords of the Jordan, and the crowds multiplied, coming from near and far to see and to hear. By common consent they thought him to be a prophet. His rugged personality, his burning zeal, and his manner of life made them think of Elijah the Tishbite, who, according to the thought of later generations, had set the pattern for Hebrew prophetism. He reminded them of that other prophet who also came from the desert of Judea, Amos of Tekoa, and who proclaimed the coming of a day of judgment and insisted on moral conduct rather than on correct family descent. Years later, when Jesus in his controversy with the rulers in Jerusalem raised the question of John's authority, his opponents could not deny John's worth for fear of being stoned, "for all held that John was a real prophet" (Mark 11:32).

The desert setting of John's life with its effect on his manner of living and thinking was more than accidental. One of the significant facts regarding the Israelite nation was the effect of the land on their thinking. Surely the story would have been different and for the worse had they lived in the luxuriant valleys of Egypt or Mesopotamia.

Palestine, particularly Judea, was semi-arid, merging closely on the east and south with the Arabian desert. The Israelites in their early formative years as a nation had been desert nomads. The greatest danger which threatened them as a peculiar people of God, when they took possession of Canaan, lay in the new luxury with its attendant vices which the economy of cultivated valleys and walled cities afforded. From the beginning the prophetic writers of the nation's history deplored the effect which the sensuous manner of Canaanite living and religion was having upon the religion and ethics of the Israelites. Not all the prophets were desert dwellers like Elijah and Amos, but there was a common opinion among them. They were convinced that the permanence and the destiny of the covenant people depended on their holding fast to the ways of the fathers rather than on exchanging them for the gadgets which the new culture offered. The prophets held to the severely simple worship of Jehovah and exhorted their people not to yield to the allurements which the native religions offered. The strict demands of the ancient Nazarite vows and the valiant example of the Rechabites, who continued to live in tents, were typical of this school of thought.

John was truly of the prophetic line, but he looked forward rather than back. He was the herald of the coming Messiah. In some superficial aspects of his life he was different from Jesus. Jesus accepted this fact when he described the behavior of the religious leaders in his parable of the contrary children.

" 'We piped to you and you did not dance;
we wailed, and you did not mourn.'

For John came neither eating nor drinking, and they say, 'He has a demon'; the Son of man came eating and drinking and they say, 'Behold, a glutton and a drunkard, a friend of tax collectors and sinners!' " (Matthew 11:17-19). John tended to be ascetic and solitary; Jesus was more sociable. John's manner of life in its severe simplicity was much like that of the Essenes, with whom he was probably acquainted since some of their colonies were located in his home territory. He was a Nazarite, which meant more than that he let his hair grow long and did not drink wine. This symbolized for him his rejection of the luxurious and his adherence to the severe manner of life which the prophets defended. This simplicity was a matter not of necessity but of choice. Mark describes his dress and food as follows: "Now John was clothed with camel's hair, and had a leather girdle around his waist, and ate locusts and wild honey" (1:6). He was not "a man clothed in soft raiment" (Matthew 11:8). He belonged to the common people, as did Jesus. He was not concerned about his personal fortune, but he had a passion for the will of God and for righteousness.

For John the Kingdom was not political or nationalistic, but it inhered in the relation of the individual with God and with his fellow man. The Jews, though the covenant people, must repent if they were to gain admittance into God's favor. John was not a revolutionist as were the Zealots; his preaching was not a call to arms, but to repentance. It is true that he stressed the apocalyptic idea of the Kingdom to be ushered in on the great Day of Jehovah, but this conception of the Kingdom differed from that of Jesus in degree of emphasis rather than in fact. Jesus did not reject the apocalyptic but was able to harmonize the sudden and catastrophic idea of the Day of Jehovah with the Kingdom growing from within.

John was no weakling, no pale ascetic, but a man of strong personality who swayed men by his bold personality and prophetic abandon of emotions. Though he was the herald of the Servant of Jehovah, his whole mien was that of strength. His customary greeting to the crowds which came was "You brood of vipers! Who warned you to flee from the wrath to come?" (Luke 3:7). It was not that he was disdainful of people. His passion was for the glory of a righteous God who was just now fulfilling his promise of the Kingdom. This favor was for God's people, but the holiness of God was so terrible that men could find his favor, not because they were children of Abraham, but by a change of life. "Bear fruits that befit repentance . . ." (Luke 3:8).

In the further fortunes of his life and its end, he was to share a like fate with Jesus. Though he was accepted by the multitudes with great warmth and devotion, he was opposed by the Jewish leaders and became a victim of Herod. Carrying on his work for the most part in Perea, he escaped the threat of the Great Sanhedrin, though the Matthew and John gospels agree that Sadducees as well as Pharisees from Jerusalem came down to look him over. The Pharisees could not have been pleased at his unorthodox ways of preaching, and the Sadducees were alarmed lest his activity affect their political fortunes. He may never have visited Jerusalem, but that he was well known to the multitudes is shown by the incident which occurred during the Passion Week (Mark 11:27-33). But the religious leaders did not accept his person or approve his message. They were of the same temper as their fathers, who killed the prophets of old. John's insistence upon the fundamentals of righteousness rather than outward forms and his straightforward speaking of the truth rather than the use of smooth words were certain to estrange these dignified persons, if they were not already rebuffed by his rude "brood of vipers" (Matthew 3:7; Luke 3:7), which included them.

As in the case of Jesus, the real danger to his life came from the political rulers. Herod Antipas may not have been as ruthless and cruel as his father; he relied more on shrewdness than on outward action to secure his ends, as is witnessed by Jesus' reference to him as "that fox" (Luke 13:32). But political rulers are ever jealous for their reputation and power, and they make short shrift of anyone who in any fashion challenges their authority or speaks in critical fashion. The political ruler's concern is always for his reputation and the permanence of his power. Friends are rewarded only so long as they serve; opponents are ruthlessly liquidated.

The gospels tell the story of Herodias and Herod's adulterous marriage with her. Josephus, who pays rather high honor to John, states that Herod feared a popular uprising which might affect his security. This does not contradict the gospel account. It is a foolhardy thing to criticize a monarch. The prudent man keeps his mouth shut in evil times. Elijah took his life in his hands when he dared to condemn Ahab, and particularly Jezebel. Though Herod had his better side and was attracted to the prisoner in his dungeon and "heard him gladly" (Mark 6:20), yet when he was forced to a decision through the tricks of Herodias he sacrificed an innocent man rather than lose face with his companions. Do not blame Herod; the politically conditioned man cannot act otherwise.

The prophets stressed ethical behavior above the meticulous observance of cultus which a settled economy tended to bring in. The simpler religious ceremonies of the days in the desert gave way to cultus and elaborate temple buildings, and all this was helped along by a corrupt priesthood. The prophets had long before John insisted that it was not enough to belong to a chosen people or to multiply sacrifices. What Jehovah required was "to do justice and to love kindness, and to walk humbly with your God" (Micah 6:8).

And surely there is no reason to pity John in his going; he shared the common lot of the prophets, who are never in honor among their own people. Only later generations build monuments to them. What Jesus said of John—that "among those born of women there has risen no one greater than John" (Matthew 11:11)—has been attested by thoughtful men of all ages; Herod is remembered only as a pitiable example of weakness and political ambition caught in the snares of a woman even more ambitious than he. No one wastes a tear over his later disgrace and banishment.

So John in both his life and his death conformed to the Servant pattern, which Jesus was to assume and carry through to complete fulfillment. The true spirit of the man is shown in his complete unselfishness. When his disciples showed a partisan spirit and complained that Jesus was stealing honors which belonged to John, he replied that it was as it should be. "He must increase, but I must decrease" (John 3:30). John has not received the attention and honor which he deserved, not through any lack of greatness, but because he was overshadowed by the Coming One, who was greater than he, whose herald he had the honor to be. John was truly great because he made himself a servant.

CHAPTER FOUR

The Call of the Servant

"Thou art my beloved Son; with thee I am well pleased" (Mark 1:11).

Whatever the convictions regarding his ultimate life's work which may have come to Jesus during the hidden years—and there were many—whatever the influences which finally sent him out into his public ministry, it is evident that the urge of these forces came to a culmination at the time when he met John the Baptist. From the gospel records we learn that the public ministry followed almost immediately upon that event. Mark records the simple statement, "In those days Jesus came from Nazareth of Galilee and was baptized by John in the Jordan" (1:9). This meeting and his baptism, together with the phenomena of the coming of the Spirit and his hearing of the voice from heaven, were the immediate circumstances which conspired to draw Jesus from the quiet life of a carpenter, with its opportunities for study and meditation, out into a ministry to his people from which he would not return. That chapter of his life was finished.

But we must not suppose that the course of his life was determined wholly by the outward and objective. There is a mystic side to the life of every man, and God is able to speak through his Spirit with a voice not audible to the physical ear. God may be in the wind and the earthquake and the fire, but he speaks more surely through the still small voice. What is true of ordinary humanity was eminently true of the unique person, Jesus Christ. In his case, the only limitations lay in his essential humanity. He did grow in intelligence; he needed to study and to meditate; he must search for the will of God. Yet we must believe that he had abilities beyond those of the best of mankind, and we cannot declare confidently that his commission came as a formal document or that he needed a theophany to realize God's purpose for him. The hidden years had been years of preparation; his moral harmony with God, his instinctive grasp of spiritual truth, his periods of meditation and prayer prepared him for that hour when he must begin a new chapter of his life. Therefore the full realization of his destiny did not come as a surprise.

The reports concerning the strange preacher at the fords of the Jordan had reached Galilee as well as nearer localities, and Jesus joined the crowds who journeyed to see and hear this person who had attracted so much notice by the strangeness of his manner of life and his striking personality, as well as by his announcement that the kingdom of God was near at hand. It was not the superficial curiosity of the careless, but the sincere interest of the deeply religious, that brought Jesus to John. We cannot know for sure that there was anything between them more than the kinship of sincere souls, both deeply concerned about God's purposes for his chosen people and for the world. This may well have been their first meeting. It is true that their mothers were kinswomen, according to

Luke. But their widely separated places of residence and the hermit type of life which John preferred would make a former meeting less likely. Jesus probably went to Jerusalem occasionally to attend the festivals, but we have no hint that John ever left his desert home to visit the capital city. John remained in the desert till he was ready to preach to his people, and then he did not go to the cities but to convenient spots in the desert of Judea where water for baptism was to be found. The statement in the John gospel, "I myself did not know him" (1:31), is not conclusive against a former acquaintance, for he is clearly referring to Jesus' claim of Messiahship rather than to personal acquaintanceship. On the other hand, John's acceptance of Jesus' superiority as recorded by the Matthew gospel (3:14, 15) does not necessarily depend upon an earlier knowledge on John's part. He may well have come to this conviction as the result of extended conversations with Jesus on the occasion under review.

Though John and Jesus seem not to have been much alike, their differences were superficial as compared with their agreements. John was convinced that God was about to move again in human history, to take a further and decisive step in his program for lost mankind. With this Jesus agreed. "The Kingdom of God is at hand" was the theme of both John and Jesus in their preaching. They read its coming in the disturbed political and social conditions of the times, in the foregleams of the prophets. The spirit which had inspired the prophets moved them as well. They agreed that the Kingdom would be neither political nor based on material fortunes; it was to be a spiritual regime. Righteousness from within rather than outward pretensions, either of wealth or race or class, constituted its essential demand upon those who would share it. John's expectation was primarily eschatological; the Day of the Lord with its terrors and splendor was about to dawn. For Jesus the approach of the Kingdom was more subtle and gradual; the Kingdom would come quietly like the growth of a seed sown in the ground. It would be as leaven, transforming both the individual and society from within. But Jesus did not reject the apocalyptic. It was always in the background of his thinking, not as something contrary to, but in harmony with, the concept of inward growth. The fullness of the Kingdom would come in the end by a direct act of God.

The record of the meeting of the two is very brief. We must allow a measure of play of the imagination to supply some of the details. One fact stands out clearly—there is no hint of disagreement, of jealousy on the part of John, or of criticism or condescension on the part of Jesus. There must have been extended conversations concerning that which was on the hearts of both, the coming of the long-awaited Kingdom of God. Of all the sincere persons who had come to hear John and accept his baptism, there had been none like this visitor from Nazareth. John could not fully sense the beauty and majesty of the personality before him, but surely the meeting with Jesus was the crowning moment of his life.

Jesus approved John's ministry. Months later he praised John before the crowds when he asked the question, "What did you go out into the wilderness to behold? . . . A prophet? Yes, I tell you, and more than a prophet" (Luke 7:24, 26). He showed his approval here when he asked to share in John's baptism. Sincere Christians have always found a difficulty in this act. Why should one, who seems to have been without consciousness of sin in his life, insist on baptism? John's baptism was one of repentance unto remission of sins; all the accounts agree on this point. The Matthew gospel records the tradition that John held back, declaring his unworthiness to administer baptism to one purer than himself, but that Jesus insisted: "Let it be so now; for thus it is fitting for us to fulfil all righteousness" (3:15). It was the will of God that Jesus be baptized. He did nothing outside that will, and so John must acquiesce.

But the will of God was not for Jesus an arbitrary command; it was something consistent and rational, in agreement with God's purpose for his life. We cannot fully understand the mystery of the Incarnation, and surely the idea that the God-man should assume the humble role of a servant is beyond our full comprehension. But what may seem to us to be not fitting may not have been so in the mind of Christ. The mind of man does not agree with the mind of God. Paul declared that the gospel of the Suffering Servant is foolishness to those who are perishing. According to all the records, there seems to have been nothing incongruous in the act, nor was there any sense of disagreement with his consistent sense of moral harmony with God. His sense of moral perfection was not that of the religionist of his day who could pray, "God, I thank thee that I am not like other men" (Luke

18:11). Such a one would not have submitted to John's baptism of repentance.

The Pharisees did not heed John's preaching. The Luke gospel declares that "the Pharisees and the lawyers rejected the purpose of God for themselves, not having been baptized by him" (7:30). Those who arrogate to themselves a great name, be it religious or political, are too proud to take a lowly position which would identify them too closely with the masses of men. Kings and war lords, and perhaps bishops and popes, hold themselves above what is imposed upon common men. To confess need of absolution would be a confession of weakness and would endanger the prestige so necessary to their position.

But the Servant had no such false pride. His sinlessness did not need to be advertised in the temple, nor did its preservation demand that he separate himself from the defiling company of the common people. The people who accepted John's baptism were in the main sincere, but they were of the lower class according to the rating of that day. Their clothing was not rich; patching seems to have been a necessary art in those days. Jesus did not shrink from such company. As far as casual observation went, he was apparently not different from the others.

His act was not for mere show, according to the pattern of the cheap political trickster. It, like all the acts of his life, was performed out of sincerity. But if the dominating motif of his life was that of the Servant, his conduct must be in keeping with that motif. It is true that this act was not in agreement with the popular pattern, but there is a constant contradiction throughout the whole story; the

Incarnate Son of God took the form of a servant, being born in the likeness of men. He who was forever separate from men shared the baptism of men.

It was in the events which followed immediately after the baptism that the climax of the occasion came. The synoptic gospels agree that God spoke directly to him as he came up from the water. The vision of the Spirit descending as a dove and the hearing of the divine voice were intended primarily for Jesus. Only the John gospel indicates that the experience was shared by the Baptist. Whether the experience was objective or largely subjective makes little difference. At this point the call came in full tone to Jesus to take up the work of God's Anointed, and he accepted it as God's commission. "Thou art my beloved Son; with thee I am well pleased" (Mark 1:11). The first line is a quotation from Psalm 2. In the Luke text, some manuscripts add "today have I begotten thee" (3:22, footnote). This psalm was regarded by the Jews as Messianic, and to Jesus the words suggested that he was to play the distinguished role of the Anointed One. The second line is from Isaiah 42, one of the great Servant passages of Isaiah. The Jews had not attached Messianic significance to the Servant section of Isaiah, possibly because the idea of king and slave do not agree. But for Jesus there was no incongruity—rather, the Servant motif set the pattern for the Messianic role which he accepted from this day forward. Thus the call of Jesus came not in a vision of marching armies or of pomp and glory of inaugural ceremonies. It came in an hour of humility when he shared with the multitudes the baptism of John.

CHAPTER FIVE

The Servant Faces His Task

Jesus said to him, "Again it is written, 'You shall not tempt the Lord your God'" (Matthew 4:7).

The experience of Jesus at the fords of the Jordan had stirred his soul to its depths. His orders had come. God had called him to be the Anointed of Jehovah, the long-expected Redeemer. There could be no doubt in his mind; he had not misinterpreted the experience. The words which had come to his heart and ears were his commission. He may have had earlier experiences which pointed this way—inner stirrings or even a vision. But now the hour had come. And full of the wonder which that hour had brought, he had gone away from John and the multitudes on the banks of the Jordan. But it was not back to the familiar scenes of Nazareth; he might go back there presently, but not to stay. His commission sent him to every part of the homeland, to Galilee and Judea, and even to Samaria. But he was not yet ready to meet the crowds. When the time came, the Father would give the word. When that day came, he must face his task with no clouded vision, with no doubt that he was fully in the will of God. During the quiet years at Nazareth he had thought deeply upon God's redemptive purpose as it was being worked out through Israel. Perhaps he had felt a growing urge to throw himself into the struggle, but an unseen force held him back.

But now the call had come to him; he was the Anointed One. With it came the sobering thought that God was moving anew and in unique fashion into history, not as of old through lawgiver and prophet, but through one who was in unique fashion a Son. With this realization there came an imperative sense of need to go apart from men into a quiet place where he could face his task and see clearly the path before him. It was not a question of acceptance. His devotion and close harmony with God which had developed through the years had made compliance with God's will natural to him. There was no holding back as in the case of Moses, no running away as with Elijah. But still he must tarry. He needed added strength to carry the burden which had been thrust upon him. The task was a mighty one, beyond any task ever imposed upon men. He, like those whom the world has ever called great, had not been called to impose his authority on men. He was to be the Servant, the one who would lift the burden of sin which crushed mankind. This sense of responsibility was made all the keener by doubts whether his people would respond. They had hoped for a deliverer who would sit upon a throne, a warrior who would command armies, rather than one who would assume a humble role. This expectation of his people seemed so reasonable, and he was so much a part of them on the side of his humanity, that he was assailed with doubts as to whether the role of the Servant was the will of God. There would be many crises in the days to come, even to Gethsemane and the cross. But perhaps the hour of decision when he faced his mission was the most momentous of all, and upon it hung the success of God's plan and the destiny of mankind.

Grave questions challenged him: Could he be assured of acceptance with his people? Would his program receive their approval? The hope of a golden age had been in the minds of the Hebrews for centuries. Their religion had been looking forward to the day when the goal would be realized. They had looked forward to political independence, to material prosperity, even to world domination. Though the dream had often seemed impossible of attainment, the desire and hope still burned fiercely in the heart of the nation. The brief period of independence under the Maccabees, after the nightmare of Gentile oppression which culminated in the cruel persecution by Antiochus Epiphanes, had raised anew the fever of patriotic hopes.

It was a time of a new and rabid nationalism. Once content if they could only live their lives in their own little land without interference from their neighbors, the Jews now had new dreams of splendor. Were they not Jehovah's covenant people, destined to rule the world? This nationalism held them in its grip. The time was near when God was about to fulfill his promises, made long ago to Abraham. "Salvation from our enemies and from the hands of all who hate us; to show mercy toward our fathers and to remember his holy covenant" are words typical of the literature of that day. God would send into the arena of the world his Messiah, a glorious person, with all the resources of heavenly power at his command. When the Day of Jehovah dawned, when God moved to restore his people, then neither the might of Rome nor the demonic forces of Satan could prevail. It would be a day of material abundance; the earth would produce her fruits ten thousand fold, and no longer would the hungry go unsatisfied.

"They shall plant vineyards and drink their wine,
and they shall make gardens and eat their fruit"
(Amos 9: 14).

In that day the yoke of the Gentiles would be broken; the Messiah would rule the nations with a rod of iron. All this Jehovah would bring to pass.

There were different opinions as to the means God would use. Some, particularly the Zealots, were out-and-out revolutionists. They plotted to fight against Rome by force of arms and were waiting only for a leader to encourage and command. It may appear to readers of history that this was even less than a forlorn hope, but not so with the Zealots. With God on their side, nothing was impossible. Had not Judas Maccabee with a handful of courageous men "put foreign armies to flight" (Hebrews 11:34)? In the famous valley of Bethhoron he had won a more notable victory than that of Joshua (see Joshua 10:11) when Jehovah fought for Israel with hailstones.

There were others who, under the spell of the apocalyptic literature of the past two centuries, believed that God, in his own time, would intervene in human history through a heavenly Son of man, and with angelic armies destroy the enemies, both human and demonic, of God and Israel. Those who held to this expectation would wait for Jehovah to move, for vengeance belonged to him. But they were more than complacent spectators of the coming drama; they hated the enemies of Israel with the same fierce hatred.

There was a faction among the Jews, not many in number but influential, who believed that the political fortunes, particularly of those in power, could best be preserved by making friends with their Roman overlords. This philosophy had existed among the Jews for three centuries and had been a real influence from the days of the Greek domination. The political rulers of that day, who were the priests, had succumbed to Hellenism. The writer of 1 Maccabees complains that the priests neglected their duties in the temple to attend the games in the gymnasium. Ashamed of the badge of Judaism, they attempted to erase the mark in the flesh—circumcision. They adopted the Greek hat, the symbol of citizenship in Antioch. This movement later took form in the sect of the Sadducees, who in the days of Jesus were in control of the temple and of the Great Sanhedrin. They were willing to compromise and give up some of the distinctive tenets of their ancient religion for selfish benefits.

Jesus knew well these trends among his people. They were dressed up in terms of patriotism and religion and were in line with much of their nation's thought of earlier centuries. But his instinct for truth led him to look beneath tradition to the underlying threads of God's revelation, to search beneath the accretions of dross for the pure lode of gold. It was not disloyalty to his people that he put all things under scrutiny and review, judging not according to human opinion so largely affected by local and superficial considerations, but according to the will of God.

But his problem was not one for easy decision. There was always the temptation to follow the philosophy dear to the hearts of the leaders of this world, to further their own interests by giving the people what they wanted. Why be a martyr, like the prophets, when he could win acceptance by going along? Or would not the end justify the means? This is a thought that has intrigued even the best of men. If he estranged the people, would he not be doing disservice to God? These popular fancies made their appeal to Jesus; he had inherited the traditions of the Jews. This made it difficult for him to combat the popular expectations. He was tormented with the thought, as all the prophets had been, that the will of God lies somewhere in the range of popular opinion. (See Jeremiah 20.) Should he not become a Messiah according to popular expectation, not only for the sake of his own reputation but also because this might be the will of God? Should he set up his judgment against that of his own people, especially since they were no common clay but the covenant people of God? Were they not the congregation, the *ekklesia,* of God? The infallibility of the church is a tenet hard to deny or oppose.

But his instinct for truth challenged every human reasoning, however plausible it might appear. The hour was too important to go forward without a complete rethinking of God's purposes for mankind. He must be true to his highest revelation. He must not decide upon the basis of convenience or upon any temporal or spatial consideration, but upon the basic will of God, even though such an action would cut across all traditions.

So he went into the desert for meditation and decision, and the struggle was so intense that for a time he neglected to eat. The desert was a waste of rocks and sand, a land of little water and scant vegetation except in the rainy season. It was sparsely inhabited, being occupied by shepherds and their kind, who wrested a meager living out of any unfriendly soil. Jesus went without food forty days, but not because it could not be secured in the desert. He was absorbed in interests more important for the moment than concern for the physical, and so set aside the appetites of the body. He was not miraculously sustained, and he must have emerged from the experience terribly emaciated. Matthew and Luke agree that "he hungered." His hunger prompted the suggestion that it would be possible and proper that he convert a stone into a loaf of bread. The superficial resemblance between the two would help the suggestion. Jesus used it in a parable later when he said, "Or what man of you, if his son asks him for a loaf, will give him a stone?" (Matthew 7:9).

This temptation to create bread had a double application, to himself as an individual, and as it related to his official role; to satisfy his own hunger, and to set a pattern for the Kingdom. The temptation was a subtle one, in that what was suggested was not in itself wrong; barley bread is not an evil but a good thing. Jesus was not an ascetic. Hunger was not a blessing in itself; nor was the body something evil to be punished. But Jesus rejected the suggestion for two reasons:

First, it was not ethical to work a miracle for his own benefit. It was not consistent with the role of the Servant that he put his own interests first. He was sharing the common fortunes of mankind, whether good or bad, and to have demanded special privileges would have put him into the class of kings and rulers, and out of class with the common run of men. Those who serve cannot but suffer privation.

Second, he found the answer to that other question: Should he use his powers to supply the physical needs of his people on a large scale? Hunger is a terrible thing, and his people had their full share of it. It was not an evil thing which Jesus was tempted to do. On the contrary, we who live in the knowledge of the physical hunger and even starvation among millions around the world may well feel that to feed them is an imperative. "Let other things wait until this be done," we say. But the instinctive good judgment of Jesus rejected this materialistic conception of the Kingdom. God spoke to him through the Scripture, saying that "man does not live by bread alone . . ." (Deuteronomy 8:3), and later he himself would say in a similar context, "Instead, seek his kingdom, and these things shall be yours as well" (Luke 12:31). Man was designed to be more than an animal, and his highest good cannot be secured by providing only food and shelter.

A few observations may be in place here. Note that the temptations have this formula, "If thou art the Son of God." This class of conditional sentences allows the condition to be fulfilled. Jesus assumed that he was the Son of God, the Anointed One, and these suggestions to action were based on that premise. We are not to assume that there was an objective appearance of Satan; the story is cast in the mold of the apocalyptic language of that day. Jesus believed that any suggestion contrary to the highest will of God came from Satan, the archenemy of God. But this experience was no doubt subjective, as were most of Jesus' experiences; theophanies are not frequent in the record of his life. Further, these temptations were not to immoral and sensuous sins. They related to the pattern of his contemplated ministry and constituted a choice between the lower but more popular opinion and the higher and more severe will of God. What was suggested had the appearance of good and could even be supported by Scripture texts. The difficulty lay in choosing between that which was respectable, but misguided, and the best, which rested on the knowledge of the will of God.

The temptation to use violent force to secure his ends and those of the Kingdom came to him. It was in Galilee that the Zealot movement arose. In the year 6 A. D. there was a revolt under Judas of Galilee, who resisted the enrollment imposed by Rome, and at this time the city of Sepphoris, near Nazareth, was destroyed. (See Acts 5:37.) Jesus was well acquainted with the Zealots and their continued plotting against Rome. To us it would seem to be the height of folly, granted that it was not unethical. But to the Jews it was within the range of possibility. Their faith that God would fight their battles rested upon their early history when Jehovah was presented as the great war god. This concept of God had been renewed as late as the Maccabean period. The question of inadequate power was not raised, for God was all-powerful. Jesus later was assured that he might secure from the Father more than twelve legions of angels (Matthew 26:53).

But Jesus was able to rid himself of his cultural inheritance. For him the objection to the suggestion lay not in the inadequacy of power but upon moral grounds. The operation of the power of God was limited by moral considerations. The Kingdom of God could not be set up by violence. The law of the harvest has never been repealed: that is reaped which is sown. Violence cannot produce peace, nor can destruction bring plenty. The forces by which the Kingdom was to be set up were not material but spiritual, not destructive but constructive and life-giving. The Jews were largely dominated by hatred for their enemies, the Gentiles, who, they believed, were also enemies of God. They reasoned that God would act in accord with what men thought best. Thus the Kingdom of God could be established when their enemies were destroyed. This thesis has always seemed reasonable and good, even to this late day in history. Even Christian nations, so-called, today can find no way so effective to establish democracy, world peace, and security as war.

But Jesus could not share this view, though rejecting it meant going against much of the thought of his people. The will of God lay elsewhere. To follow that will would be a slow process and neither easy nor popular. There would be a cross at the end of a road full of misunderstanding and opposition. Already he sensed something of the tragedy which his decision involved. He had come to cast fire on the earth, and he shrank from the conflagration, not for himself but for his people, who were faced with making a fateful choice for which they were not prepared. But the road he chose to follow was the right one; it was the only plan that could succeed. For hatred must be substituted love, and for violence, service. The sword would not bring in the reign of peace. It would not only fail, but to use it would be to worship Satan and dishonor God.

Then came the temptation to do the spectacular. If he were to go to the temple at a feast time and leap from the dizzy height of the pinnacle to the pavement below without harm he would capture the admiration of the crowds. Was he not the Son of God and could he not claim special favor? Did not the Scriptures promise God's protection?

"No evil shall befall you,
    no scourge come near your tent.
For he will give his angels charge of you
    to guard you in all your ways.
On their hands they will bear you up,
    Lest you dash your foot against a stone" (Psalm 91: 10-12).

This would be an acceptable sign to the people. They believed that the Messiah would give some such demonstrations. Later they would ask Jesus for "a sign from heaven," something more spectacular than kind words and physical cures. The human loves the spectacular. It is still good advertising copy. But the sensitive soul of Jesus shrank from such an exhibition. The Servant must not put himself forward by any kind of trickery, but must be true to his nature. He had no lack of trust in God; God was ready to keep him in all his ways. But the Servant could claim no special privilege. He must share the common fortunes of mankind and be willing to be last rather than first. To claim special privileges would be presumption.

Here, incidentally, is a good sample of Jesus' use of Scripture. Had he used the common proof-text method, perhaps he would have yielded to the suggestion. But he always went beneath the letter to find the unified and consistent purposes of God. So although the psalm suggested itself to him in the phrase, "It is written," he found a deeper and more basic word in "Again it is written, 'You shall not tempt the Lord your God' " (Matthew 4:7).

It was not easy for Jesus to reject these suggestions which were put forward and approved on the basis of patriotism and religion. He was a Jew, with a deep devotion to his people. It was only because of his complete devotion to the will of God and his instinct for truth that he took time to view the whole matter objectively, rather than to move upon impulse. He could not be satisfied with patriotic shibboleths. How they are substituted for reason! In the end his search was rewarded. The instinct which would not be satisfied with less than the full will of God led him to reject decisively all these compelling suggestions. Through the years he had been building a pattern based on certain basic assumptions regarding God and his redemptive purpose; he found these suggestions at variance with that pattern. The Servant pattern was revolutionary because it went contrary to human reasoning.

The human pattern demands a show of outward authority and power. It exalts human pride and pins its faith to the material rather than the spiritual.

But the Servant pattern was not new in the sense that it was not contained in the previous revelation of God to his covenant people. It had been a precious thread running through the fabric. The Scriptures had been written by men inspired but influenced by their cultural patterns. Therefore the idea of a strong political kingdom had always played a prominent part in their expectation. The monarchy established by David had become an ideal. It was only gradually that a higher vision emerged, particularly in the prophets. None of the writers of the Old Testament were so free from nationalistic bias as the prophets. And it was the prophets, particularly Jeremiah and the writer of the Servant section of Isaiah, who inspired the deepest thought of Jesus. These writers dared to rise above the lower level of the national to that universalism which was implicit in monotheism, that cultural tenet of Judaism. It was the prophets who brought monotheism to the fore. They wrote in the time of the dissolution of the state when hopes for the future were at the lowest point. It looked as though the covenant people were engulfed in the common ruin which the rise of imperialistic states had brought to the small nations. The promises of a glorious future for the Hebrew people, given first to Abraham, the father of the nation, seemed to have gone by default.

When Jeremiah advised his people to surrender to the Chaldeans, he did it in no sense of futility. The plan of

God for his covenant people was not defeated by this turn in their political fortunes; it could go forward under a new covenant, built on a surer foundation (Jeremiah 31:31-34). But it was the writer of the Servant section of Isaiah who rose to new heights of vision and daring. In a series of Servant songs interspersed through chapters forty to fifty-three, he brings a message of consolation to a people crushed by the disasters which had befallen them. He deals fearlessly with the question: Had God abandoned his people when he gave them into the hands of a pagan nation? It is significant that the English translation of *goyim,* the Hebrew word for *nations,* begins at about this point to use the word *Gentiles* to express a new shade of meaning. The word was used as a term of derogation; the world was now divided into two groups, Jews and non-Jews. The Gentiles were thought of as *hamartoloi* (full of sin). They were regarded as without God and as agents of Satan.

The writer of this section of Isaiah comes to grips with the problem with directness and daring. He assures Israel in captivity that God is neither impotent nor forgetful and that his purposes for his people will be carried out. They shall conquer the Gentiles, but it will be a bloodless conquest. If blood is shed, it will be theirs and not that of their enemies. Israel is to adopt a new role, that of a servant.

It will be a humble role (42:2):

"He will not cry or lift up his voice,
or make it heard in the street. . . ."

Israel must give up her selfishness (49:6):

"It is too light a thing that you should be my servant

to raise up the tribes of Jacob
and to restore the preserved of Israel;
I will give you as a light to the nations,
that my salvation may reach to the end of the earth."

It will be a role of humiliation (53:2):
"For he grew up before him like a young plant,
and like a root out of dry ground;
he had no form or comeliness that we should look at him,
and no beauty that we should desire him."

He is pictured as one whom men thought to be under the wrath of God (53:4):
". . . yet we esteemed him stricken,
smitten by God, and afflicted."

But victory is promised to the Servant (49:7):
"Thus says the Lord,
the Redeemer of Israel and his Holy One,
to one deeply despised, abhorred by the nations,
the servant of rulers:
'Kings shall see and arise;
princes, and they shall prostrate themselves. . . .' "

The Servant is Israel, the remnant who were carried into exile because of the sins and failures of worldly minded rulers, who turned a deaf ear to prophets like Isaiah and Jeremiah and persisted in their mad course. But the message of the prophet here is one of comfort and promise for the future. They shall fulfill God's plan for them to bring his salvation to the ends of the earth. A world held by demonic forces of sin was to be redeemed.

This could not be accomplished by violence of war or by political scheming. These were often used to place added burdens on men's shoulders and to push them deeper into despair. They were a part of Satan's equipment. Even law and education and all other corrective methods devised by men, though good, were not adequate—there must be service and love and even innocent suffering and shame and death.

"By his knowledge shall the righteous one, my servant,
make many to be accounted righteous;
and he shall bear their iniquities" (Isaiah 53:11).

This was the vision of the prophet. It was perhaps never popular though it should have brought courage to the Hebrew captives beside the watercourses of Babylon. In the time of Christ this quiet voice of prophecy appealing to the heart of the nation was drowned by the cries to high heaven for vengeance on their Gentile overlords. The Jews now believed that they were destined to sit upon the throne of the world. According to some of the apocalyptic writings, nothing short of destruction of their enemies in Gehenna would satisfy them.

But there were those who kept the vision alive in their hearts, patient souls, the poor in spirit who were waiting for the consolation of Israel—not for material benefits or political power, but for a reign of righteousness broad enough to include all men.

CHAPTER SIX

The Servant's Claims

"I am the way, and the truth, and the life; no one comes to the Father, but by me" (John 14:6).

The temptation in the desert was over; the devil had departed for a season. Jesus had reassured himself that he had not been mistaken—he was God's Anointed, but in special fashion, a servant rather than a king. He was ready to begin his work. John had been imprisoned by Herod Antipas and Jesus would not seem to be competing with him. So he turned to Galilee, his home country, to begin his work. It was to be a mission of proclaiming the good news of the Kingdom and of healing the sick.

What would be the reaction to his mission? Would the people understand what was in the mind of Christ, and, if so, would they respond? If he held God's promised salvation in his hands, then it was imperative that they understand him. To receive his benefits, it was necessary that men have a faith concerning him, as well as a faith in him. Was he only a great man, like one of the fathers of Israel? Was he a second Judas Maccabee? Or was he more than a great man? "Who do you say that I am?" is a question that is still pertinent. Every thoughtful Christian will attempt to go back as near to Jesus as he can and stand with those who companied with him, to look upon his face and hear his words, to observe the manner of his life, in order to learn God's secret which he had entrusted to this person.

As Jesus embarked on his public work, what was his thought about himself? What he thought about himself may seem to disagree with what men would like to think of him. But his reputation and his worth do not depend on human opinion; he is above human judgment. It is not for us to dictate the pattern of his life but to seek that vision that will enable us to see in him the full flowering of God's character and redemptive purpose.

There are two obstacles to our finding the mind of Christ. If we believe that he was the Incarnate One, how can we understand him? We have difficulty understanding men; how then one who is more than man? It must be more than an intellectual analysis; rather, a process of spiritual revelation. Then too, the problem is made the more difficult in that he did not make his claims of authority and mission openly. He was the Servant and as such he could not vaunt himself and openly put forth his claims to greatness, lawful though those claims were. He would not cry, or lift up his voice, or cause it to be heard in the streets (see Matthew 12:17-21). He was compelled by his role to be unassuming and meek, even to the appearance of weakness. This was God's way, God's plan for him. If this appears strange to our human minds, we must remember that the fault lies with us, "for the foolishness of God is wiser than men" (1 Corinthians 1:25). But to those whose hearts are open in faith, he is divine power and divine wisdom.

What was God revealing through him? Was Christ

only a man, good and wise beyond all others? He was this, but more. As we contemplate him, we are driven to the conviction that he was unique, apart from and above all men.

First, is his moral character. In this he was separate from his fellows, even those who were most noble. He accepted the tragic fact that all men, even the best, are sinners. But he himself betrayed no sense of guilt. The Pharisee whom he described praying in the temple was a good man according to his own light. Jesus did not make him a willful liar, but rather one who was sadly mistaken about his true condition and who because of this foolish belief in his superiority was guilty of self-righteousness and contempt for his fellows. He received no answer to his prayer, not because he was without need, but because, being blind to his glaring faults, he asked for nothing. It was in no such spirit of boasting that Jesus set himself apart from other men. It was, rather, out of a feeling of complete harmony with his Father throughout his whole life. And there was nothing incongruous in this role he had taken; moral goodness is not enhanced by boasting or advertisement—instead, it is tarnished. As we contemplate his life we find no hint of sin or moral imperfection. There are many recorded instances of Jesus' praying. Nothing in his life was more impressive than his prayer life, but we seek in vain to find him, either in word or attitude, asking for forgiveness. We do not need a proof text such as "Which of you convicts me of sin?" (John 8:46). His perfect religious instinct, his complete devotion to God's will, and the power of the Spirit produced a life that was perfect and without blemish. He never said "our Father," but "my Father" and "your Father." Even when he spoke of God, he was apart from men.

Second, he was unique in his perfect instinct for truth. He was not educated according to the standards of modern science, he was not learned in the Greek philosophy of his day, nor had he been trained in the scribal schools of the Jews. He was not a *grammateus,* a man of letters. His critics were astonished at his grasp of religious matters, since they knew that he had had no formal training. He was not versed in the so-called Oral Law, the traditions of the elders. But in the field of the moral and spiritual he possessed a knowledge of the truth of God which went beyond that ever attained by man. The limitations of his humanity compelled him to seek this knowledge, at least in part, through study and meditation. His practice of quoting from the Scriptures as the Word of God is evidence of their importance to him. Doubts assailed him, as is the case with all men. He was tempted in the desert to follow the popular pattern, and this temptation would recur again and again. But his passion to follow the will of God and his instinctive grasp of truth kept him from being satisfied with anything less than the full counsel of God. He could truthfully say, "I am the way to God, because I possess the truth."

Third, he was unique in his official relationship with God; he believed that he stood in a place apart from and beyond all men in the working out of God's redemptive purpose. There had been a long and glorious line of men through whom God had spoken, "the fathers," as the

Jews lovingly called them. Jesus was in this line of succession. He declared that he had come to fulfill that earlier revelation contained in the Law and the Prophets. His was a prophetic mission, but it is an understatement to speak of him as the greatest of the prophets. His was a priestly mission; he had come to bring men into the presence of God, but he was more than the greatest of high priests. This is the theme of the letter to the Hebrews. His authority went beyond that of any man. He was not only the perfect revelation of God; he was unique in that God had put the destiny of mankind in his hands. Paul expressed this faith when he wrote, ". . . to unite all things in him . . ." (Ephesians 1:10).

This uniqueness finds its explanation in the mystery of the Incarnation. Though Christ was entirely human, he was also divine. There was that plus factor which even the best of men do not possess. The Christian church believes he was more than human because he regarded himself as such. Only one who was more than man could be the Savior of men. To such a one alone could God entrust his plan of salvation. And without appearing presumptuous and never forsaking the humble role of the Servant, he believed that he was God's Anointed One. He asserted at the risk of being called a blasphemer that he had authority to forgive sins. The Pharisees contended rightly that this was not a human prerogative, but he insisted that "the Son of man has authority on earth to forgive sins" (Matthew 9:6). He promised forgiveness to the woman in the house of Simon (Luke 7:36-50) and salvation to the repentant thief (Luke 23:43) and to the house of Zacchaeus (Luke 19:1-10). In the synagogue at Nazareth he declared that the Messianic promise of Isaiah 61 was being fulfilled in him. He offered rest to the heavy laden and declared that "the Son of man came to seek and to save the lost" (Luke 19:10). And whatever content of humility he put into the title, Son of man, he did use it also in terms of authority. He spoke of the Son of man coming on the clouds, of sitting on the judgment throne. He declared that he could ask the Father and he would grant him more than twelve legions of angels.

This uniqueness of character and power was moral and spiritual, and not in the area of material and political power. From a human standpoint he possessed little of those things which men prize highly. He shared the fortunes of the lower classes. He left the carpenter shop in Nazareth to embark on the precarious profession of an itinerant teacher. Truly he could say that he had no place to lay his head. The only property he possessed when he came to die was the simple clothing he wore.

How did Jesus make known his designs to men? He was the one to whom God had entrusted the Messianic salvation, and God had planned to do it through a servant. All the means of propaganda which seem so necessary to the world were set aside when God sent his Son into the world with none of the trappings of power. How could men be brought to believe on him? And yet faith in the Saviour of the world was necessary. How were they to know that the promised salvation had come? They expected the Messiah to come with marching armies, or on the clouds through opening skies. They expected portents and signs from heaven to herald the advent of the deliverer. How could they see the Coming One in the Nazarene, who neither possessed nor cared for that which the world prizes most highly? The king, the military leader, the great ones of the earth announce their claims by royal proclamations. Our modern world is conversant with the ballyhoo of the political leader, the advertisements of big business, the claims of this cult or that. Even religious people are not above sounding a trumpet through the streets.

But the Servant must be true to his calling. He who was above kings and all the great ones of the earth claimed no earthly authority. He who was offering to men the treasure above all the treasures of the world accepted poverty as his lot. He did not claim honor but chose to efface himself, accepting instead scorn and misunderstanding, even the shame of a Roman cross. On one occasion even his own brothers twitted him for his self-imposed modesty (John 7:3-4). When his disciples finally could say, "You are the Christ," he strictly charged them to speak to no man concerning this (Mark 8:29, 30).

Why did he behave thus? Was he not hiding his lamp under the measure? If the knowledge of him was so vital to mankind, why did he not announce it openly? From the human standpoint his behavior in this respect was unreasonable. It is only when we get a true perspective of the Servant role, when we lay hold, in a measure, of spiritual vision, that we begin to see strength instead of weakness in his effacement. The place of miracles in establishing his claims will be discussed later; it is sufficient to say here that they did constitute signs, though not the only ones. They were wrought out of compassion rather than from a desire to shine. The important fact in the present discussion is that Jesus attempted to escape the applause which followed the miracle. Again and again he charged those whom he healed to tell no one. He would not allow the demon-possessed man to speak, "because they knew him" (Mark 1:34). On only one occasion did he bid the cured one to tell his story (Mark 5:19). But this exception is explained by the fact that the incident occurred outside Jewish territory where it was not his intention to tarry.

This reticence on Jesus' part has had different explanations. One is that Jesus was cautious and so attempted to prevent attracting too great notice to his ministry. If he became widely known, opposition would develop more rapidly and endanger his life and mission. There was danger of this, it is true. Herod became curious when he heard of the new prophet who was also a wonder worker, and the curiosity of a Herod was not without danger. Too great popularity would also assure greater opposition from the religious leaders. Jesus was not foolhardy; he charged his disciples to flee when they were being persecuted, and he did exercise a measure of caution for himself, but not to the degree that would mark him as a coward. He did the will of God, and, when the time came, he went to the cross without regret.

Another explanation is that he was attempting to limit his healing ministry in favor of his spiritual ministry, that this is the reason he refused to return to Simon's house the morning after the great day in Capernaum. This contention has point; he was more concerned for the spiritual than for the physical and material. Sympathetic as he was toward all the woes of mankind, he always kept in mind the distinction between the material and the spiritual.

But the basic reason for his self-effacement is this—only such behavior was in keeping with the character of the Servant of Jehovah. The Servant could not be other than humble and self-effacing. Pride and glory belong to the kings and great men of the earth; that is the pattern of the world. The true glory is not that of the outward; it is within, in the graces of character, in service and love. His was the true humility—not ignoble, not a fawning mask assumed for unworthy motives. He rejected praise and ran away from fame because it was distasteful to his sensitive spirit. It was the humility of the "strong Son of God," who needed no artificial bolstering of his self-respect. By refusing honor, he made himself more honorable. By refusing worship on earth, he made himself worthy of divine worship by his church. One of the most relevant quotations in the Matthew gospel is from Isaiah 42:1, 2, quoted in Matthew 12:18, 19. Jesus had been healing sick folk and, as was his wont, he charged them to tell no one. The gospel writer said that it fulfilled the words of the prophet:

"Behold my servant, whom I uphold,
    my chosen, in whom my soul delights.
I have put my spirit upon him,
    he will bring forth justice to the nations.

He will not cry or lift up his voice,
or make it heard in the street."
This is the one in whom the nation shall hope.

But it was not Jesus' purpose to hide the truth about himself. The light came not to be placed under the measure or under the bed, but on the stand. "The true light that enlightens every man was coming into the world" (John 1:9). But the light must be revealed in true fashion. It was contrary to the character of the Servant to make open claims. The evidence was not in outward show, but in those virtues and graces which were embodied in him. His claims were not put forth openly to the public after the manner of worldly proclamations; they must make their impact on the consciousness of men through the beauty of his character, his words of grace, the strength of his love and compassion, the sense of his saving power. In him there was a haunting sense of God's presence as when human eyes catch vistas of beauty and ears seem to hear strains of heavenly music. Sometimes the light of his divinity broke through the veil of flesh. In the story of the unexpected draught of fishes, Simon Peter cried out, "Depart from me, for I am a sinful man . . ." (Luke 5:8). The truth must be revealed not in human fashion, by "flesh and blood," but from God, who hides the truth from the wise and prudent but reveals it to babes.

It was by incidents from his life and by words quietly spoken that his character and claims were revealed. Perhaps we see him in the light of history, through eyes which have been opened by faith. The careless multitude then as now missed these revelations, as even his own disciples often did. Their senses were attuned to the disputes of the market place, to the pomp and show of the world, to the specious promises of political leaders, rather than to the meekness of the Servant. But he was speaking, in his loving service to the weary and heavy laden, in the beauty of his spirit which shone through in every word and gesture.

Sometimes Jesus spoke more openly. On one occasion he said, "No one knows who the Son is except the Father, or who the Father is except the Son and any one to whom the Son chooses to reveal him" (Luke 10:22). These words remind us of the John gospel, in which Jesus is made to speak his claims more openly. Yet in this gospel he declares, "If I bear witness to myself, my testimony is not true; there is another who bears witness to me, and I know that the testimony which he bears to me is true. . . . for the works which the Father has granted me to accomplish, these very works which I am doing, bear me witness that the Father has sent me" (John 5:31, 32, 36).

CHAPTER SEVEN

The Authority of the Servant

"Tell us by what authority you do these things, or who it is that gave you this authority" (Luke 20:2).

The above title is a seeming contradiction in terms, but the whole gospel is paradoxical. Paul spoke of the foolishness of the cross. The claims of Jesus to a place of unique importance are not reasonable, and the Incarnation is a mystery. Had the Incarnate One come with all the trappings of pomp and power, he would still have been difficult to understand, but men would have been more inclined to accept him. Had he taken on the glory of the apocalyptic, evading the door of the flesh in his entrance into the world, coming on the clouds with the angels, his acceptance would have been easy for those who belonged to the apocalyptic school. But the road of the Incarnate One was the road of humiliation. Paul saw this clearly when he said, ". . . who, though he was in the form of God, did not count equality with God a thing to be grasped, but emptied himself, taking the form of a servant, being born in the likeness of men" (Philippians 2:6, 7). In the Incarnation not only was the divine shrouded by a veil of flesh but his lot was cast among the lowly of the earth. There was no intention on the part of God to bolster up the material and social fortunes of his Son; rather, it was by God's design that he shared the lot of the lowly, for was he not called to be the Servant? The Christ could not company with kings and rulers but, rather, with the poor and obscure. The story does not read like that of a king but like that of a peasant and slave.

The things which made him unique were not in outward appearance. The moral excellence of his life, his sinlessness, was not readily apparent among a people whose best men sounded the trumpet of self-righteousness, whose purity was outward and ceremonial rather than of the heart, who could thank God that they were not like other men (Luke 18:11). His inerrant comprehension of moral and spiritual truth, which enabled him to find the will of God perfectly, was not appreciated by the men of his generation who had made over their God according to their own desires. And regarding his official relation to God, to be the deliverer of Israel, who could regard such a claim seriously since he refused to make his claims publicly? And had he done so, his manner of life was not one to inspire the respect and trust of his people, who were expecting a political and military deliverer.

That the men of his day were slow to see beyond the human and commonplace in him is not strange. The senses of humanity are attuned to the stimuli of the world. Man's materialism is a curtain which all too effectively shuts out the light from beyond his physical orbit. The Christ's reception was not favorable. The common people were attracted by his miracles and stirred by his teaching; to many, his complete dedication to the cause of religion marked him as a prophet. They thought of him as John the Baptist risen from the dead or as Elijah or one of the prophets. But even those who were friendly did not understand him perfectly. The gospel writer could truly say, "He came to his own home, and his own people received him not" (John 1:11). This unfavorable reception is shown in the murderous anger of the leaders in Jerusalem, the outraged cries of the religionists, and the growing disappointment of the common people, who wanted bread and cures.

The impasse was so great that only spiritual forces could overcome it. No one can come to the Christ "unless the Father . . . draws him" (John 6:44). It was to those whose hearts were responsive to the Spirit, whose wills were subjected to his will, that there came a dawning consciousness of the unique in Jesus, a knowledge which was more than intellectual, an awareness of the presence of the divine. It was not easy to describe or put into rational terms, but beyond human attainments in him they saw something more, a plus factor, elusive and yet real, like a fleeting dream hard to recapture, a flash of color, a haunting strain of music. Many must have sensed this uniqueness in him, but could not analyze it. It caused their hearts to burn; it spoke to their consciences; they seemed to catch faint glimpses of divine glory. Simon Peter could speak in familiar fashion to his guest in the fishing boat, but, amazed by the miraculous draught of fishes, he cried out in awe, "Depart from me, for I am a sinful man, O Lord" (Luke 5:8). Though they could not describe it in words, they felt the impact of his personality, a compulsion on their affections. When the crowds listened to his words as he taught the great truths of the Kingdom, they sensed an authority greater than that of their scribes. The people of his home town, Nazareth, though full of prejudice against him, could not help but marvel at the words of grace which proceeded from the mouth of the carpenter's son.

But this was not the dust-dry authority of the schools, not the regimentation of lives by a dictatorial government, not the curt orders of the military saying, "Do this or that." It was a sense of spiritual compulsion akin to that of God. His authority was demonstrated by his influence on men's lives, an inward compulsion which the Nazarene wielded on all who met him. Zacchaeus, in the presence of perfect goodness and warmed by his guest's friendliness, caught a vision of what the Kingdom of God was like, and, under the urge of the desire to be close to Christ and retain the vision, he cut loose from his selfishness and cheating. He could never go back to the old life—it had lost its charm. He now had a new sense of direction and values. The sinful woman in the house of Simon the Pharisee (Luke 7: 36-50) felt in his presence a poignant distaste for her past life, so tawdry and empty, and found a power to attain to something new and beautiful. She could never be the same again; she had come under the compulsion of the Nazarene. And many others, whose names and stories are not written on earth, humble folk for the most part, found in him the deepest desire of their hearts—vision and power to transform their lives.

But not all responded to the high call to repentance and the higher life. Some felt the impulse but were bound by alien forces too strong to break away from. The rich man who came asking the way of eternal life could not break away from his prison house of wealth; he felt the compulsion keenly, and though he refused the counsel of Jesus he went away with a sense of distaste for his former life and of frustration which would haunt him to his death.

Others, bound by selfish desire for station or entrenched in smug respectability, resented the challenge of the Galilean to the pattern of their lives. Such a one was the demon-possessed man who cried out in resentment at Jesus' interference, "What have you to do with us, O Son of God?" (Matthew 8:29). Evil men like Caiaphas and his crowd were resentful at his condemnation of their nefarious business and confronted him with the challenge, "By what authority are you doing these things . . .?" (Matthew 21:23). They were smarting at his mastery of the situation. Their clients in the temple, selling birds and animals, and changing money, had made a spectacle of themselves, running away from the unarmed Nazarene. On an earlier occasion the Sanhedrin had sent officers to arrest him and were chagrined when they came back empty-handed with the preposterous excuse, "No man ever spoke like this man" (John 7:46). They were embarrassed at this question regarding the authority of John the Baptist; caught between their contempt for the Baptist and their fear of the crowds, who held him in high esteem, they had to evade the issue, lamely saying, "We do not know" (Matthew 21:27). They could not respond to his teaching and counsel; it would have changed them from caricatures into real Israelites without guile; it could have saved the city and temple from destruction.

However, they could not be indifferent to him and his demands. To all appearances he was only a religious enthusiast with a motley group of followers. He had no material power, no political prestige, no army at his back. Why did he drive them to such desperate action? They ordinarily paid scant attention to men of the servant class. Was it not that they recognized in him an authority greater than theirs? They stood convicted before him, and they thought to free themselves by plotting his destruction.

What was the secret of this strange power which the Servant held over men? As stated before, it was not material force, nor the authority such as the state wields. He had no such power had he desired it. His authority was spiritual, the moral authority of God through the perfect medium of the Incarnation. He was the revelation of God, of his righteousness, truth, and love. Sinners in his presence saw themselves as in a mirror, but the vision also brought hope; they found salvation. Men who were groping, who had lost their way, found a clear path, an answer to every despairing question. Men who were helpless in the grip of evil forces found new powers in the life he offered. He was indeed the way to God because he possessed the truth and the life. The secret of his authority lay in those things which made him unique—the moral perfection of his life and his perfect instinct for truth. These were qualities of the Incarnation, the instrument of God's redemptive purpose. By a strange paradox this authority was in direct ratio to his humility. It was the Servant of Jehovah who compelled the conscience and heart of mankind. Had he come as an earthly king he could have wielded power over men's bodies alone, and that only for a time. But the Servant wielded his power over the spirits of men.

And the Christ still walks on the earth today, challenging his followers to heroic deeds for his name's sake. He speaks to men at the busy crossroads of life, saying, "Follow me," and they turn their backs on what before had seemed all-important and follow him, going in the spirit of the Servant to the dark places of the earth. He rebukes men for their sins: those high priests of religion who care only for their prestige and advantage; the merchants of the business world who use their power over men's lives to increase their wealth, no better than the rich men of Amos's day who sold "the righteous for silver, and the needy for a pair of shoes" (Amos 2:6); the political and military leaders who bow down to the idols of nationalism, attempting to build their fortunes upon the blood and tears of war's helpless victims. Christ has become the conscience of the world. Not all men follow him, but they must reckon with him. In order to ease the pressure, men often attempt to bring him to their side, trying to make him an ally rather than a judge. Nations pray for victory in war in his name. Many men would be happy to believe that their riches have his benediction. Others would excuse their sensuous living with the plea that he was liberal in these matters.

But he cannot be coerced. He will not fit into any pattern which men in their arrogance make for him. The Servant speaks with the authority of God, and men hear him speaking either for weal or for woe. He was sent not only to administer God's redemption, but to vindicate God's righteousness. "For judgment I came into this world, that those who do not see may see, and that those who see may become blind (John 9:39). And though the nations may flaunt his words and crucify him again and again, there will come a day "when the Son of man comes in his glory, and all the angels with him . . ., before him will be gathered all the nations . . ." (Matthew 25:31-32).

CHAPTER EIGHT

The Stern Demands of the Servant

"This is a hard saying; who can listen to it?" (John 6:60).
He went away sorrowful (Matthew 19:22).

There is a popular but superficial picture of Jesus that represents him as "a hail fellow, well met," one who entered fully into the activities of men, even those of a lighter and doubtful nature. It seems to be fairly popular to defend certain social practices on the ground that they were of the kind of things in which Jesus took pleasure. It is true that he mingled with all kinds of people, and, more often than otherwise, those of the lower social stratum. *Publicans, harlots,* and *sinners* were common terms of reproach applied to them by the social and religious elite. "But this crowd, who do not know the law, are accursed" (John 7:49).

Jesus was social; he loved people for themselves and he loved them because they were the objects of his redemptive concern. There was a social side of his nature, but that is not the whole picture. He was "a man of sorrows and acquainted with grief." He came as the Servant of Jehovah to lift the burdens of lost men. The Servant could not be self-indulgent or careless. He walked a toilsome road and at its end there would be a cross. He broke his heart over the spectacle of the world—mankind bewildered, stumbling, bound, and blinded by Satan. He grieved at man's inhumanity to man, the sorrows of the poor, and the complacency of the rich and powerful. He wept over the cities who rejected his gospel, over Jerusalem and its coming destruction, over the temple, his Father's house, which was desecrated by an unworthy priesthood. He was also assailed with doubts as to the rightness of the Servant role. There was a joyous side to his nature, but a somber one as well.

The joyousness of Jesus' life was in contrast with that of John the Baptist, who preferred the solitary life. But it is a slander to suppose that Jesus sought men to partake of their sins, or that he was careless in his behavior; he was not social in that respect. His happiness and well-being did not depend upon the noisy clamor of feasts. If he lived in our day he would not be an addict of night clubs. He did not lower himself to the level of men, nor was he dependent on men to set the pattern of his life. His pattern cannot be likened to any human pattern, however lofty. He moved in a realm above men, for he was more than a man. He was concerned not to be like men but like God. His morality was not the mores of his times. He gave himself to mankind, but at the same time he kept himself apart from men. The true picture of Jesus was that of One who followed a higher leading immaculate in its perfection, yet the Servant of Jehovah sent to redeem men.

There was of necessity an inner core of reserve in his life, a reserve which only those who were spiritual sensed. That he shared the excesses of men or found pleasure in them is the grossest slander. He was called "a glutton and a drunkard, a friend of tax collectors and sinners" (Matthew 11:19) by his opponents; in saying, this, however, they were willfully malicious, unless they were blind to moral truth. But often today, not in malice but to find a cloak of respectability for that which is unworthy, men who name his name assert that Jesus set the example. He is even dragged into our so-called "holy" wars, but the only uniform he is willing to put on is the garment of a servant.

The secret of his conduct in seeking sinful men was not to share in their sinful deeds but to save them from those deeds. His every act was redemptive; in the face of this there can be no hint or suspicion of levity. He never abandoned the role of the Servant—grave and sorrowful, yet tender.

The Pharisees who accused him of keeping unworthy company had an exaggerated sense of their own superiority. Their concern lest they be defiled by contact with those of a lower social stratum amounted to a phobia. It was a selfish and misguided concern for their own reputation. Because they were victims of a faulty system, they were unable to understand his conduct. It was his love and concern for lost souls which made him seek out men, both high and low. He had no fear of ceremonial defilement; that was an imaginary danger. Man can be defiled only from within, and that with a moral defilement. The purity and high purpose of his life preserved him from moral taint. He was free not only from the sensuous sins of the lower classes but also from the selfishness and bigotry of the so-called upper classes.

But though Jesus was social, he kept himself under strict discipline. His religious instinct had led him to take the high road. He could not be satisfied with the ordinary, nor did he stoop to deceit and casuistry to cover up shortcomings. He lived a life of perfect moral purity, not because he was unable to sin, but because he was able not to sin. He was "one who in every respect has been tempted as we are" (Hebrews 4:15) and who in order to overcome temptation was able to lay hold on spiritual powers.

He was not easy on himself; his life was one of stern discipline. Nor was he easy in his demands on those who would follow him. He rejected men who were not willing to count the cost. To the men who thought the Kingdom would afford honor or material benefits, he declared that he did not have them to give; ". . . the Son of man has nowhere to lay his head" (Matthew 8:20). He refused to allow another to stay to bury his father and to put on a farewell party. There would be crosses to bear. "If any man would come after me, let him . . . take up his cross and follow me" (Mark 8:34). The rewards of the Kingdom are so great that a man does well to make any sacrifice in order to secure them. No price is too high to pay.

But the demands of Jesus are not arbitrary; they are reasonable and consistent with the nature of the Kingdom. If the road of the Servant led to the cross, then his disciples must be willing to carry crosses and follow him. They will rejoice to share the toil and the hardships and the shame of their Master; ". . . it is enough for the disciple to be like his teacher, and the servant like his master" (Matthew 10:25). Consider further the words of Jesus: "If any one comes to me and does not hate his own father and mother

. . . yes, and even his own life, he cannot be my disciple" (Luke 14:26). "Unless you turn and become like children, you will never enter the kingdom of heaven" (Matthew 18:3). "No one who puts his hand to the plow and looks back is fit for the kingdom of God" (Luke 9:62). "Do not be anxious about your life, what you shall eat, nor about your body, what you shall put on" (Luke 12:22). "And there are eunuchs who have made themselves eunuchs for the sake of the kingdom of heaven" (Matthew 19:12). Was Jesus teaching asceticism? No, not in the sense that the physical and material are to be regarded as evil, and holiness to be attained only through severity to the flesh. But Jesus demanded that men lift their lives above the sensuous. There are other and higher values than the material, and even the lawful demands of the physical must be kept in subordination to the spiritual.

The life to which Jesus called men was indeed rigorous, but it does not follow that it would be joyless. There were other hardships which his followers would be called to endure for his sake. What were these demands?

Jesus declared that the gospel might easily bring division into the closest of human relationships, the family. He said he had come to bring not peace but a sword. It had so happened in his own case; by heeding the call of the Father and obeying his will, he had estranged his family. This was not by his own desire or devising; it came as the result of his commitment to a higher allegiance. However, the gospel will not always bring strife and separation. It will enrich and sanctify every human relationship when all the members of the family respond to it.

But there are forces opposing the Kingdom of God and these, unless they are sternly repressed, will produce opposition and division even in the home. In that case, he who would follow the higher allegiance must renounce earthly ties and commitments.

To choose to walk the high road is not easy. It is difficult, not only because it runs counter to the physical urges within men, but also because the issue is often clouded. There are many voices calling in this world, wooing men to follow them. They are not unmasked in their evil intent; they are voices of men who themselves are bewildered, walking in darkness and following a will-o'-the-wisp which lures them, not to safe paths but deeper into the morass. Men who have only the light which their humanity affords walk at best in the twilight. Man was not created to walk alone by his own intelligence. At his best he needs illumination from outside himself, the light which comes from his Creator. Without that light, he confuses values and may defend what is secondary, or positively evil, as objects of his first devotion.

It may be that in his ignorance man strives to make Jesus the sponsor of his plans and actions. There are many phases of our modern life, economic, social, political, which present their programs for the approval of men, clothing their appeals in high-sounding terms. They may even drag in the name of the Lord in support of unworthy ends. He is made to sponsor economic schemes, all the way from capitalism to socialism. War is represented as a crusade in his name. But Jesus sponsored no forms of evil; he supported no particular form of government or economic plan. He set forth the great eternal truths of God; he announced the high ethical demands of God. But these demands were never easy; they were absolutes. In his life and teachings, men may find wisdom to create social patterns which promote justice and brotherhood. It is only as men follow him who is the light of the world that they can see clearly the high road and have courage and power to walk in it. For Jesus set no easygoing standards.

Jesus insisted, "Do not lay up for yourselves treasures on earth . . . but lay up for yourselves treasures in heaven. . . . For where your treasure is, there will your heart be also" (Matthew 6:19-21). Treasure is that upon which a man depends for life and happiness; therefore it is imperative that man rest his life on that which is permanent. "You cannot serve God and mammon" (Matthew 6:24). Denoting any form of the material, *mammon* is an Aramaic word derived from the verb for *to trust*. Jesus saw the rich utterly dependent on their wealth for their happiness and security. The possession of material wealth has a subtle danger for all men; we are all earthborne creatures, whose physical life depends on the material. If we were physical only, well-stalled oxen, then our highest good, the much-desired security, would consist of food and shelter, of luxury and pleasure. The Epicurean philosophy, "Let us eat and drink and be merry," has always had its appeal.

But man is also a spiritual creature. So he finds a battle raging within himself, his lower nature striving to dominate the higher. Paul made famous this conflict between flesh and spirit. No one ever resolved this conflict perfectly except Jesus, and he alone saw the situation with a clarity beyond human perception. In the light of this perfect vision, he made stern demands upon those who would follow him, even to the point of abandoning wealth and cutting loose from the demands of the flesh; ". . . if your right hand causes you to sin, cut it off and throw it away . . ." (Matthew 5:30). Without doubt Francis of Assisi was regarded as simple-minded by his neighbors when he embraced a life of poverty, but history regards him as the greatest saint of his day.

The door into the Kingdom is difficult. "Strive to enter by the narrow door; for many, I tell you, will seek to enter and will not be able" (Luke 13:24). Man is limited by human imperfections. He is enslaved by the forces of sin. However, these seemingly impossible demands which Christ put upon discipleship are not arbitrary or unreasonable; they are necessary if men are to become free. And he promised a power, beyond the human, whereby men could throw off the shackles of the old life and become new creatures. Paul said that "if any one is in Christ, he is a new creation . . ." (2 Corinthians 5:17). So, in paradox, that which was impossible has been made possible by the enabling grace of God.

CHAPTER NINE

The Miracles of the Servant

"He took our infirmities and bore our diseases" (Matthew 8: 17).

A familiar description of Jesus' ministry is found in the following text: "And Jesus went about all the cities and villages, teaching in their synagogues and preaching the gospel of the kingdom, and healing every disease and every infirmity" (Matthew 9:35). This is but one text out of many, and they all agree that his ministry to the people always included acts of healing. Miracles of healing are found throughout the story and are among the better remembered material. The healing of the centurion's servant, the raising of the widow's son at Nain, the restoration of the Gadarene demoniac, the feeding of the five thousand—these are typical of the wonder-worker. In this Jesus showed the true spirit of the Servant.

His compassion upon all suffering would not allow him to pass by with unconcern anyone who was in pain or need. Wherever he went, he found sick folk. In the crowds who gathered to hear the prophet from Galilee were many who came both to hear and to secure cures, for Jesus had the reputation of being both a prophet and a wonder-worker. John had attracted large crowds by his dynamic preaching, but the one who came after him worked wonders in addition. Perhaps the impulse to heal came and went. In the story of the paralytic carried by four men

(Luke 5:17-26) it is stated that "the power of the Lord was with him to heal." The word which is translated *miracle* is the Greek word for power, *dunamis*. When the sick woman in the crowd took hold of the tassel of his garment, Jesus perceived that power had gone from him.

The working of miracles was regarded by the Jews as a special gift of God bestowed on men. Paul spoke of the gift of healing as one of the gifts of the Spirit (1 Corinthians 12:9, 28). In the Old Testament there are cycles of miracle stories, one in connection with Moses, and a second in connection with Elijah and Elisha. When Jesus raised the widow's son from the dead, the multitude rejoiced that "a great prophet has arisen among us" (Luke 7:16). It was a commonly held belief that Messiah, when he came, would perform many miracles (2 Esdras 13:50). There was intense interest in miracles in Jesus' day. This interest was intensified by the great need for help among the people.

Though the science of medicine had been known for a long time among the Greeks, there was little knowledge of it in the lands immediately east of the Mediterranean. There was an almost total ignorance of sanitation and of medical science. Any hint of such knowledge said to be found in the Law is probably to be explained on the basis of the ceremonial and religious rather than that of the scientific. Lepers were driven out from society in order to prevent ceremonial defilement; it is true that unwittingly by such procedure they may have prevented the spread of the disease. But in most cases pestilences spread through the people unchecked and finally waned through lack of victims. Those who professed to be physicians were either charlatans or men who in skill and knowledge were little above the medicine men found among primitive peoples. The woman who had suffered many things at the hands of many physicians is a case in hand. Many people were too poor to afford even the questionable help available. The lame beggar at the Beautiful Gate of the temple (Acts 3) and Lazarus at Dives' door (Luke 16) are examples of the abject helplessness which was so common.

The interest in miracles was increased by the belief that many diseases, if not all, were the direct penalty of the sins of the sufferer, imposed by God. A later thought was that Satan sent them as a part of a nefarious curse which he worked on men (Luke 13:16). Therefore the cure of disease became a religious act, rather than a scientific one.

The study of miracles, particularly those of Jesus and his followers, poses a problem for our age of science. Miracles were accepted phenomena in the ancient world, but in our day they are looked at askance. The ancients believed that their God would interfere at his pleasure in his world, either through human agency or without. God was interested in mankind and if necessary would interfere in his world in objective fashion. Men knew nothing of a universe operated by natural law which is so fixed that the mere thought of interference is regarded as foolishness or even heresy by the scientists of our generation. Therefore the miracles of Jesus, which were once regarded as an important if not the chief proof of his Messiahship, are now not only a minor ground of faith but even a stumbling block to it.

Many moderns seem to feel themselves under compulsion to rationalize the miracles. They assume that miracles cannot occur in a well-regulated universe. A common answer to the problem is that the ancient belief in miracles is but superstition and that it is good to be educated out of it. A more kindly explanation is that there was no miracle but that what was at first only a startling event or act grew through much retelling into the proportions of the miraculous. For instance, this treatment of the story of the feeding of the five thousand: in spite of the fact that the place was desert and far removed from a town, they found to their great surprise that there were ample supplies when they pooled their resources. Thus the story is worked over to teach sharing, rather than the compassion of our Lord. Through the exaggeration incident to much retelling, a striking yet reasonable event becomes a miracle.

A more common modern definition of a miracle, and one which is more charitable toward the ancient world, is that a miracle is the result of the operation of natural forces, the existence and operation of which are at the moment unknown to the observer. With the coming of greater knowledge, the miracle is seen as a natural phenomenon. This preserves the inviolability of natural law. Certain of the miracles of Jesus seem to yield themselves to this treatment.

It is interesting that the particular class which is regarded as easiest to explain today was to the men of that day the most difficult — demon possession and its cure.

Demon possession was regarded as the worst calamity which could befall men, and the most difficult to cure. The Seventy, when they returned from their mission, rejoiced that "even the demons are subject to us in your name" (Luke 10:17). Modern minds reject the idea of the existence and activity of demons, and easily diagnose the so-called demon possession as a form of insanity, aggravated by their belief in the existence and evil activity of demons. Jesus, it is explained, was able to release the sufferer from fear; when the fear of demons was taken away, the demon was gone and the victim was cured.

In our attempt to understand and interpret the gospel story, we need to be cautious lest we read back into it our more advanced (so-called) knowledge. We must agree that for the writers, and for Jesus himself, miracles were regarded as a direct activity on God's part. That was sufficient explanation for those who believed that God was at the center of the universe as its creator and sustainer. He was personally interested in mankind and would bind up and heal as well as punish. He was a God "who heals all your diseases" (Psalm 103:3).

We need, rather, to remember that it is difficult to eliminate all the objective supernatural from religion and have any substance left. An honored teacher of the author frequently said that everyone accepts some of the miraculous. In times of great danger, the most sophisticated is driven to pray that God will do the impossible. Further, we have not fully explored the realm of the spiritual, nor do we know all its laws. That there are real spiritual forces which make their impact on the material and physical cannot be confidently denied. God is not interfering in the so-called miracle; he is but using laws of his own making which are unknown to man.

Beyond these technical questions regarding the existence and *modus operandi* of miracles there are certain aspects of the matter which are closer to our main thesis, the miracles of the Servant. Certain conclusions are evident.

First, Jesus worked no miracle, nor did he do anything else, merely to astonish men. They were often astonished, but that was the result, not the purpose, of his actions. He was tempted to do spectacular acts. He was repeatedly asked to give "a sign from heaven," something more than the utilitarian cures which he performed. Jesus refused with indignation any such suggestion. He resisted the temptation to jump from the pinnacle of the temple. Anything spectacular, calculated to advertise himself, was cheap and utterly repugnant to him. This reluctance to notoriety runs all through the record; often, when he performed a cure, he would say, "Tell no man."

Second, Jesus refused to use his powers for his own benefit. He shared with humanity its common hazards and asked no special dispensation for himself. Even when he had fasted to the point of emaciation in the desert, he refused the suggestion that he turn a stone into a loaf of bread. He used his powers for others, not for himself. Thus he differed from the great ones of the earth who lord it over their fellows and demand special privileges.

Third, in his miracles, as in every phase of his life, he was constructive and redemptive. He performed no punitive miracles, even to combat his enemies. No one was stricken with blindness as in the case of Elymas, the sorcerer. His cures were wrought out of his compassion and in the spirit of service. He could not look upon human misery unmoved. He held no narrow views of human suffering as always a judgment of God; that belonged to an earlier age, but it was still present. He did not dismiss the righteous judgment of God, but he held that much of suffering was the result of Satan's activities. He accepted the commonly held belief regarding demon possession and other working of Satan. He spoke of one person as "a daughter of Abraham whom Satan bound for eighteen years" (Luke 13:16). When the Seventy rejoiced that even the demons were subject to them, he replied, "I saw Satan fall like lightning from heaven" (Luke 10:18). The widespread misery of his people drew heavily on his love and compassion. What he accomplished in his short ministry may seem small when compared with our modern medical science which deals with diseases in wholesale fashion, carrying on a program of prevention as well as of cures. But it is his spirit which has inspired this program of health and healing. It is when the physician is coldly scientific, or uses his skills for fame and self-aggrandizement, that its values for the greatest good for man fall into insignificance and lose all merit when compared with the ministry of the Servant, who out of compassion gave himself freely. In this area, as in all of his ministry, he lived according to his basic assumptions – the value of human personality and God's concern and love. When we see his miracles, not in isolation but in the perspective of the total picture, the minor difficulties disappear.

The nature miracles have been particularly difficult to understand. For example, what is the value in the stilling of the tempest? One thing stands out clearly: Jesus did not regard nature, even in its more violent moods, as something alien to God. This was his Father's world, and he was not terrified by the storm; rather, he slept peacefully through it until aroused by the disciples.

Fourth, the miracles of Jesus were conditioned on faith. "According to your faith be it done to you" (Matthew 9:29). The gifts of God are offered to all without distinction, but they are not thrust upon men. Jesus did not cure men against their will. The faith mentioned so frequently was belief in his power coupled with a desire to obtain the boon. It is related that on the occasion of his visit to Nazareth "he could do no mighty work there, except that he laid his hands upon a few sick people and healed them. And he marveled because of their unbelief" (Mark 6:5, 6). They refused to ask for cures and therein lay their lack of faith.

But we need to remember that miracle-working was a gift shared by many. Others before Christ were credited with this power, and Jews of Jesus' time were spoken of as being able to exorcise demons (Matthew 12:27). The apostles were commissioned to heal. Although miracle-working was not an exclusive sign of Jesus' Messiahship, in this, as in other phases of his life, he was exhibiting in perfect fashion God's redemptive love. And because of his uniqueness, his miracles must stand apart and above all others. He possessed the power in more intimate fashion. "For as the Father has life in himself, so he has granted the Son also to have life in himself . . ." (John 5:26).

Jesus was no doubt tempted to devote the major part of his energies to this ministry. Certainly there were thousands who were suffering from want and disease. On one occasion, the morning after the great day in Capernaum, the crowds filled the street in front of Simon's house; yet he turned his back upon them and went away to other towns. We may conclude that Jesus was more than a dispenser of cures. He had come to establish the Kingdom of God, and there were other interests more important than ministering to the body. The physical is important but not all-important. Man cannot live by bread alone. It has been truly said that the gospel of Jesus is concerned with all of life, but there are gradations of values, and Jesus put the spiritual above the material. It was a source of grief to Jesus that the people sought cures for their bodies but not for their souls; ". . . you seek me, not because you saw signs, but because you ate your fill of the loaves" (John 6:26). He pitied the poor and the hungry with a pity beyond that which men may know, yet he could say, "Do not be anxious about your life, what you shall eat or what you shall drink. . . . Is not life more than food, and the body more than clothing?" (Matthew 6:25).

Jesus was more than a healer of men's bodies. Had he fed all the hungry and cured all the sick, and stopped there, he would not have been the Savior of the world. If he had gone further, as our modern social gospel demands, and removed the causes of want and disease and stopped short of redeeming the souls of men and transforming them by spiritual power, he would have failed. The righteousness of God was his supreme gift. If men secured this, their physical and material needs would be supplied in the providence of God.

Jesus saw men as God sees men, burdened and plagued with all manner of woes. These may come unbidden and undeserved. There are physical conditions which come through natural processes, because of disease and the waning of physical powers, ending earlier or later in death. Physical death is the lot of all men; the consolation which Jesus held out was not a continuation of physical life but the promise of the resurrection. There were those evils which come through the activities of demonic powers; Jesus believed that some sicknesses were traceable to these agencies. Certainly we may agree that those social ills which come through man's inhumanity to man have their source in Satan. Jesus could not have been unmoved by the avarice and selfishness of the rich and powerful who preyed upon the helpless masses. Even so, he did not countenance rebellion, but urged meekness and patient endurance. He promised justice and relief, not immediately, but at the Day of the Lord. "Blessed are you poor, for yours is the kingdom of God. Blessed are you that hunger now, for you shall be satisfied. Blessed are you that weep now, for you shall laugh" (Luke 6:20, 21). He never promised immediate alleviation of want; he had no lands to give; he did not promise to take away all pain; he could not promise immunity from ill-treatment.

There are sufferings, due to human sin, which are

deserved; these must be endured as a judgment. All men, even the saints, share in the corporate sin of the world. Even the best must be ever in a spirit of contrition. But there is the great area of innocent suffering, so tragically prevalent in our world, woes brought on by war and other evil systems, ills attendant on our physical constitution. There can be some relief through kindly service, there are great humanitarian movements, and there may be miraculous interventions. But there will always be innocent suffering due to men's physical constitution and to evil and destructive forces behind the scenes. The Christian must "always pray and not give up," in faith that God is not slow to answer.

But the greatest comfort lies in looking unto Jesus, the pacemaker and perfect example of faith. In the very nature of the role he assumed, that of the Servant, he was doomed to suffering, humiliation, and death. And what he was and endured, his followers must be and endure. There was a cross and there were other crosses. The first was on Golgotha, but, in the generations to follow, his disciples were destined to bear crosses also. Let us not make the mistake of believing that we are promised ease and security. These may come in a measure as the leaven of the gospel permeates society. But if there were demonic forces fighting our Lord, they still have to be reckoned with, and there is no assurance that they will be finally conquered until the Day of the Lord comes. The role of a servant is one of suffering and poor reputation; he may expect few miracles to relieve. He must bestow gifts, not claim them as his right. The miracles of Jesus were few in comparison with the need. His followers must expect hard going. There are compensations, however; "it is enough for the disciple to be like his teacher, and the servant like his master" (Matthew 10:25). We should rejoice at every advance of medical science which prevents the spread of epidemics and brings relief from suffering. We should rejoice at new skills which ensure food and new social machinery that ensures a more equitable distribution of the world's goods. All these attainments are in line with God's will for his world.

But to demand a miracle for one's own benefit is selfish. We may pray that God will intervene to relieve the distress of others, or our own, and have faith that the miracle is possible. But a clearer vision of the Christ will lead us to put our lives into the hand of God, not demanding special attention, but rejoicing rather to share the common lot of humanity. The boon which we should most desire is that we be called sons of God. We should desire to become channels of blessings, becoming servants to minister to the needs of the world, using resources, whether their possession be miraculous or ordinary. If we become impatient, it must be at the woes of others, not because of any distress of our own.

CHAPTER TEN

The Servant's Concern for Men

"Come to me, all who labor and are heavy laden, and I will give you rest" (Matthew 11:28).

That Jesus was devoted to God is a statement which needs no argument; it is a motif which runs through the whole fabric of his life and sets its pattern. All that he was and did was with definite reference to the Father; he lived his life perfectly under God. A corollary statement is that Jesus was devoted to men. Because he was devoted to God, he must be devoted to men. It was not the other way around; his devotion to God did not spring from his devotion to men. There are two reasons for this concern. First, he came to fulfill God's redemptive plan for mankind. God was concerned about men, therefore Jesus' concern. Second, to serve men was more than a duty imposed upon him. He saw men as God sees them, in their frailty and sin and need, but also with an appreciation of their value. His passion for men took precedence over every earthly interest. The Servant was little concerned for his own reputation and earthly fortunes. He served men rather than demanding honor and preferment for himself. Only a servant could be truly concerned with men. Anyone above a servant in rank is bound to be concerned, at least in a measure, with his own dignity and position.

Jesus was a mystic. He lived in complete spiritual harmony and communion with God. His sense of God's presence, his devotion to God's will, his perfect understanding of the truth of God, all mark him as the one perfect example of the religious. He was accustomed to spending much time in meditation and prayer, withdrawing from the society of men into solitary places, staying late and rising early. There is a record of one such all-night vigil (Luke 6:12). But there is no hint that he was what so many of his devoted followers in later centuries became—hermits who thought that the highest blessing was to be found in the solitary life. He might spend hours on the mountain speaking with Moses and Elijah about his coming departure from this life, but the morning found him back on the plain, ministering lovingly to a demon-possessed lad.

Jesus' interest in men was demonstrated in many ways. One is that he sought them out where they lived. Others might demand that the people come to them. John the Baptist established himself in the desert on the banks of the Jordan, and the crowds were compelled to journey far to hear him. But the manner of Jesus' ministry was itinerant, symbolic of his passion for men. He went from city to city, to towns and hamlets. He worked not only in Galilee, but went to Judea as well. And he did not pass by or neglect the Samaritans, those unfortunate people who could never quite win acceptance by the Jews but were regarded as outcasts and aliens. Good Galilean Jews, fearful of defilement, at the festival seasons usually detoured through Perea. Jesus did not share this prejudice, because he was above prejudice. Thus Jesus' concern drove him on, making him neglectful of his own comfort. "Let us go on to the next towns, that I may preach there also; for that is why I came out" (Mark 1:38).

Jesus required no special setting for his preaching and teaching. He was no preacher who loses his sense of dignity and poise unless robed and surrounded with all the trappings of the ecclesiastical. He was no teacher who demands the Gothic architecture of a university in order to do his best work. He did not strain to assume an artificial geniality in surroundings which were simple and often rude. The Servant was at home in a humble environment. The open sky became the canopy of the temple of God. The humble cottage he made a holy place by his presence. Wherever he went with men to pray, there was the true shrine of God, and the place where he taught men the great truths of God became a schoolroom. He loved to go to the synagogue, where the Jews met for worship and instruction, but not exclusively; he was as much at home and as effective in his work in less formal settings.

He could set up a clinic in a crowded street. Sometimes he was on the shore of the Sea of Galilee in the early morning when the fishing boats with their crews came in from the night's work, and other laborers were passing on their way to shop or field. He would begin to speak in informal fashion to a few, then more would crowd around him, never in a hurry, as is the mood of the East. Sometimes as the crowd increased he would seat himself in one of the fishing boats and speak to the people standing on the sloping shore, until finally they would go reluctantly to their neglected tasks. He spoke with people by the wayside. He was a guest in the home of Zacchaeus and that of the sisters in Bethany. Sometimes he used the open court of a home for an audience room, and the people would crowd in through the door which gave access to the street. Or he would preach and heal in the streets. Sometimes his hearers numbered hundreds or even thousands; sometimes there was but one, a Nicodemus on a housetop in Jerusalem, or a woman beside a well in Samaria.

Contrary to the pattern of the world of his day, and of ours, he made no distinction between men of different social strata. The good people of his day held aloof from the common crowd, as good churchmen have ever had a tendency to do. He seemed to be even more friendly with outcasts than with reputable folk, thus earning the nickname, "a friend of publicans and sinners." He never berated the lower classes for their sins. He was more severe with the upper classes, particularly with the religious leaders. But, in truth, he made no distinction. The outcasts proved more responsive to his approach, which was resented by the socially proud. But his freedom from class consciousness is shown by his ready response to faith, whoever the person was. He was a guest in the homes of both publicans and Pharisees (Luke 5:29; 7:36; 11:37; 14:1; 19:5, 6). He saw all men in need of God's salvation and he offered it freely to all. He rejoiced that publicans and harlots were taking the Kingdom by storm, and sorrowed that "the Pharisees and the lawyers rejected the purpose of God for themselves . . ." (Luke 7:30). To be friendly toward outcasts did not seem to him a thing strange or unworthy, but the most natural thing for the Servant to do.

He was surprised and grieved that the leaders of Judaism were offended at his concern for the outcasts. Were they not committed, in principle at least, to a program of saving all the people of God's covenant? Being a publican did not make Zacchaeus one whit less a child of Abraham. If he seemed to speak more sharply to scribes than to publicans, it was to arouse them to a sense of their danger and of their unfaithfulness to their calling as shepherds of the flock. He was not class conscious when he warned the rich of their peril and said nothing about the spiritual dangers of poverty. Even in his condemnation, he was redemptive.

But his friendship for "sinners" cut across the conventional pattern of the religious leaders' thought. Their conception of religion created a chasm between themselves and the less fortunate of their people. That one professing to be a teacher should treat these people with kindness contradicted their theories of religion, burdened as they were with their obsession for ceremonial purity. Perhaps they were smitten in their consciences for their neglect of their poorer brethren and attempted to compensate by belittling this new teacher.

That his behavior was revolutionary is shown by the failure of his own disciples to understand him fully. On one occasion he caused them to wonder and to criticize because "he was talking with a woman" (John 4:27); to speak familiarly with any woman was one of the things forbidden to a rabbi. On another occasion when the crowds were thronging about him his friends went out to seize him because they thought he was beside himself (Mark 3:21). Again, his disciples tried to discourage mothers from bringing their small children that he might lay his hands on them in blessing (Mark 10:13-16). Jesus was angry at the presumption of his disciples, but he was not angry at the intrusion of the children. It was the disciples who were at fault, not the mothers.

The great ones of earth—political rulers, rich men, and their kind—must be spared intrusion and too close contacts with the unwashed and uncouth. This is the earthly pattern. The peasant cannot presume to obtain audience with the king; proper distinctions must be preserved and proper distances kept. Time is too precious for the great one to waste on humble folk. Besides, to do so would be out of keeping with the great one's dignity. And if he should deign to notice those beneath him, it is often only a pose, a trick to gain applause for himself; the politically minded man turns every occasion into benefit for himself.

But he who alone of all men was perfectly fitted to rule, instead became a servant; and he who alone was different from all men, even the best, gave himself to all without distinction of class or condition. He who alone had the ability to make distinctions made none. Men with imperfect vision, not able even to see their own disabilities, are the first to make distinctions. Ignorant of the beams in their own eyes, they make much of motes in others' eyes. But Jesus saw men as God sees men—alike in worth and alike in need. Man sees his fellows with a horizontal vision, imagining distinctions between rich and poor, between learnéd and ignorant, between master and slave. God sees men with a vertical look, which allows no assumption of superiority of one over another. Paul spoke with true insight when he declared, "There is neither Jew nor Greek, there is neither slave nor free, there is neither male nor female . . ." (Galatians 3:28).

And Jesus showed friendliness for even the lowliest of men, in spite of the fact that he was the only sinless one, who outclassed even the best of men and much more that caricature of righteousness who boasted that he was not like other men. He who by the authority of God was made higher than the kings of the earth did not boast of his high position, but gave himself as a servant out of love for lost mankind. And it was not incongruous that the Son of God should become a Son of man, a servant of all. In this way alone he could represent God in his seeking, redemptive love for sinners.

This dominant note of concern sounds throughout his teachings; it is a true expression of his central purpose to call sinners to repentance and salvation. On one occasion the sons of Zebedee were provoked to anger because a Samaritan village refused hospitality to Jesus and his company, out of prejudice against the Jews, and they asked permission to call down fire on that village. "But he turned and rebuked them" (Luke 9:55). Some manuscripts add "And he said, 'You do not know what manner of spirit you are of; for the Son of man came not to destroy men's lives but to save them.' " These words are probably additions by a pious scribe, but they are written with a true appreciation of Jesus' character. Jesus was not a killer; weapons of violence fall from his hands. He came to save, not to destroy. "For the Son of man came to seek and to save the lost" (Luke 19:10).

The Servant's concern for lost men is graphically portrayed in some of the greatest of the parables. There are three such in Luke 15, all having the same central lesson. The setting of the chapter is a familiar one: Jesus giving time and attention to outcasts. He answers the criticism of his opponents by telling three stories of lost things and the concern of their respective owners—stories of a sheep, a coin, a son. Some interpreters find certain nice distinctions between the three: *one* sheep out of *a hundred, one* coin out of *ten, one* son out of *two*. Or, the coin was an inanimate thing, the sheep had only the instinct of an animal, but the boy was a rational being and by his own choice brought disaster upon himself. But, as in all true parables, there is one central teaching. And it is the same in these three, the value which God places on mankind, value which is enhanced when danger threatens.

The parable teaches God's love and concern for all men, and this concern of God was revealed in Jesus' concern. The contrast between Jesus' concern and the disdain of the religious leaders who were his critics is portrayed dramatically in these parables, particularly in the third story. The older brother is a caricature of the religious man, self-righteous and disdainful of others. The attitude of God is portrayed by the father in the parable. The erring son who fell into the lowest depths of sin, feeding with swine, never ceased to be the son of his father. The ragged, emaciated tramp was still his son. The older son refused to rate him as a brother and called him "this son of yours," thus unwittingly voicing the central truth of the gospel. All men, however vile, are potentially sons of God, though their fellows who are higher up the social scale may refuse to acknowledge them.

The central emphasis of the gospel of Jesus is love. Jesus reiterated the ancient command, "Thou shalt love thy neighbor," and added, "But I say to you, Love your enemies" (Matthew 5:44), in the face of a tacit acceptance of the right to hate enemies. But love denies any distinction between man and man, however difficult and strained their relations and however difficult to find value in the other man. Love is based on value; where there is value, love follows by necessity. If value is denied, then contempt and hatred follow. But no one can hate that which has value. Jesus was not creating a rule, arbitrary and impossible to understand, when he commanded love for all men. He saw men as God sees men, his own creation and the object of his redemptive love. Our difficulty with Jesus' demands is that we see, not clearly, but through the mists of our selfishness and prejudice.

It must be kept in mind that the love of Christ for men does not admit them into the favor of God regardless of their response. His love was all-embracing; that was its glory. His love was potent in winning men, stronger than argument or any authority of this world. Concerning yielding ourselves to Christ and becoming a new creation, Paul could well say, "For the love of Christ controls us" (2 Corinthians 5:14). But though the gifts of God through

Christ are offered freely to all, they are not thrust upon men, nor are they available unless they are accepted.

But the question may be asked, "Is it not true that Jesus devoted himself to the Jews alone? Had he no interest in the Gentiles?" It is true that he seemed to limit his ministry to his own people. According to Matthew he charged the Twelve, when he sent them out, to stay away from Gentile centers and Samaritans as well, "but go rather to the lost sheep of the house of Israel" (Matthew 10:5, 6). He said to the Syrophoenician woman, "I was sent only to the lost sheep of the house of Israel" (Matthew 15:24). These texts are found only in Matthew and reflect the Jewish bent of that gospel; however, the evidence as found in all the sources is that his few contacts with non-Jews were accidental and casual, rather than the result of a planned campaign.

In the heart of Galilee there were Greek centers; the city of Sepphoris was almost within sight of Nazareth. Galilee was ringed about with Greek cities: on the east and north was Decapolis, a line of ten cities; on the west was Phoenicia; and farther to the south was old Philistia. He made an overnight trip to the east side of the Sea of Galilee, where the people were largely non-Jewish, but his purpose does not seem to have been evangelistic. And he suffered no great loss when the superstitious pagans begged him to go away. He had not come to carry on an evangelistic campaign. He went out of Galilee to Tyre and Sidon, but not to preach. Mark states that he stayed indoors and "would not have anyone know it" (7:24). And when by chance the mother of the demoniac child traced him out, he departed immediately. He gave her the cure, but did not follow up the opportunity to preach the gospel. This period (Mark 7:24–8:26), which has been called the Great Withdrawal, was not used for a Gentile mission. Whether he ever toyed with the idea of turning to the Gentiles, as his great follower Paul did, we have no evidence.

We may be sure that he did not remain oblivious of the great pagan world which pressed in on Palestine on every side, and that he did not regard it with indifference and contempt. The story of the centurion whose servant was sick is told in the Luke gospel with appreciation for the Gentile; ". . . for he loves our nation, and he built us our synagogue" (7:5). This is the first reference in the New Testament to the God-fearers, who were to play a very important part in the spread of the early church. They were pious Gentiles who had abandoned their own religions and embraced the worship of Jehovah; they were not proselytes and were therefore not regarded as clean by strict Jews. It was of this man that Jesus said, "Truly, I say to you, not even in Israel have I found such faith. I tell you, many will come from east and west and sit at table with Abraham, Isaac, and Jacob in the kingdom of heaven . . ." (Matthew 8:10, 11).

In the woes pronounced upon certain cities (Luke 10:13-15; Matthew 11:20-24), he declared that the men of Tyre and Sidon or even of Sodom would have a better chance in the judgment than those proud Jewish cities. On another occasion he said that the men of Nineveh and the queen of Sheba would condemn that generation of the Jews in the judgment (Matthew 12:41-42). It is true that these words were spoken against his own people because of their lack of response to his gospel, but they are implicit of Jesus' awareness of the Gentile world and of its claims upon the mercy of God.

Why then did Jesus limit himself so largely to a ministry to his own people? The answer does not lie in any indifference to the claims of non-Jews or in unawareness of God's love for all men. But there is a practical consideration. There seemed always to be a compulsion of haste upon him, because of the magnitude of the tasks and the shortness of time. Whether the period of his ministry lasted for the traditional three years and a half, or for a shorter time as may be deduced from Mark, it was a crowded ministry. It was no unhurried mission with long intervals of rest and recreation. He knew no forty-hour week, which is the pattern of our day. He might delegate certain duties to the Twelve, but the central responsibility must be carried by him. God's revelation was through the Incarnate One and him alone. The work to be done was so great and the opposing forces so strong and determined that the time was shortened. Not that he was ever thrown into a panic; he maintained his composure. When threatened by danger from Herod Antipas he said, "Go and tell that fox, 'Behold, I cast out demons and perform cures today and tomorrow, and the third day I finish my course' " (Luke 13:32). Herod was unable to cut his time short, but the hour was determined. The third day, the end of the course, was not far distant, and he must be on his way to Jerusalem, where the prophets die.

Then too, it was the will of God that he should limit

his personal ministry to the Jews. They were God's chosen people, set apart for a great mission, to be "a light to the nations" (Isaiah 42:6). He must bring his gospel to them, that through them he might bring it to the whole world.

With regard to the Samaritans, the situation was different. Here the Jewish antagonism was even stronger than against the Gentiles; Jesus did not share this antagonism. He accepted the Samaritans for what they really were, worshipers of the same God the Jews worshiped, but victims of a long-drawn-out and bitter feud between neighbors in which there was blame on both sides. Their Scripture was the Pentateuch and they had had a temple of Jehovah on Mount Gerizim. The Jews under John Hyrcanus (about 125 B. C.) had destroyed this temple, but persisted in their refusal to allow the Samaritans to worship in the temple at Jerusalem. But for Jesus, the barrier which the Jews had built up against their neighbors to the north was artificial. The Mark gospel followed by Matthew makes no mention of Samaria; in fact, they both seem to have Jesus evade going through it on the final journey to Jerusalem by sending him through Perea.

But both Luke and John make significant references to Samaria. In John there is the story of the woman at the well and there is no hint of derogation on the part of either Jesus or the author. In the several journeys between Judea and Galilee there is no hint that Jesus ever took any road other than the one directly through that area. Luke, who also possessed southern sources, has three references to these people. There is the story of the inhospitable Samaritan village against which Jesus refused to hold a grudge.

The one leper (of the ten who were healed) who pleased Jesus by his spontaneous gratitude rather than by meticulous obedience to orders was a Samaritan. One of the most beautiful of Jesus' parables, the one which sets forth the basic rule of man-with-man conduct, has for its hero a Samaritan. In this section of Luke (9:51—18:14), other incidents and teachings may be located in Samaria. Jesus had a good word for the despised Samaritans, and the Jews suffer by contrast with them. He was willing to overlook the shabby treatment he received from the villagers, but he soundly condemned the uncharitable attitude of James and John.

The incident at the well of Sychar (John 4) is perhaps the most striking of the Samaritan incidents. Though the woman took her prerogative of throwing in his face the hated name, *Jew,* Jesus was not offended, but in skillful fashion, with a bit of humor, arousing her curiosity, bewildering her with his insights, he won her complete faith and confidence. And the story closes with the woman becoming an ardent evangelist to her fellow townsmen, crying out the appeal, "Come, see a man who told me all that I ever did" (4:29). And the climax came, when not alone through her word but also because they had seen and heard, they came to believe on him. And Jesus rejoiced at their response as men rejoice at the coming of harvest.

This story becomes the setting of that great gem of truth which Jesus spoke concerning true worship. There had been a time when sanctuaries of wood and stone and curtains were in order. The sanctuary was the shrine of

God—for the Jews, in Jerusalem; for the Samaritans, on Gerizim. But Jesus brought new truth; the shadows vanish and the clear light of day shines. God is spirit, and perfect worship is in spirit because in that is reality. And by this token, any artificial boundaries by which any group hems itself in while shutting others out are forever abolished. God is the God of all men, for wherever the spirit of man is, there is a shrine of God. Implicit in the story is the universal gospel. All men, whether Jew or Gentile, whether bond or free, whether high or low, are equal in the right to partake of the grace of God.

It was this concern for men which brought Jesus to the cross. As his ministry progressed, Jesus came more and more into danger. The end of the road was in sight, but for the present he had safe conduct; his hour had not yet come. But in the face of danger, he was not thinking of his own safety and ease. He was going to Jerusalem because it was God's will. When he rode into Jerusalem amid the cheering crowds, he was not thinking of his own glory but was concerned about his people. Weeping as he rode, he burst into the mournful wail, "Would that even today you knew the things that make for peace! But now they are hid from your eyes" (Luke 19:41). When he drove the traders from the temple, it was for the honor of his Father's house. When the net of his enemies was tightening about him, he attempted to throw up a wall of protection around his bewildered and faltering disciples. "I am praying for them; I am not praying for the world. . . . Holy Father, keep them in thy name . . ." (John 17:9, 11). In the garden when he was confronted by the mob, he gave himself up without a struggle, but bargained for the safety of his disciples, saying, "Let these men go . . ." (John 18:8). On the way to Golgotha, he said to the women who bewailed him, "Daughters of Jerusalem, do not weep for me, but weep for yourselves and for your children" (Luke 23:28). Nailed to the cross, tortured and thirsty, he had thought for his mother, and he opened the doors of Paradise to his fellow sufferer.

Thus ended the earthly life of him who in life had given himself without stint for others and in death made "himself an offering for sin" (Isaiah 53:10). The end of the road of the One who would bear the sin-laden burden of men was at the cross where the Suffering Servant "made intercession for the transgressors" (Isaiah 53:12).

CHAPTER ELEVEN

The Kingdom of the Servant

"My kingship is not of this world" (John 18:36).

What a paradox! Servants do not sit on thrones; that is reserved for kings. To be a king in this world demands certain qualifications and patterns of conduct, and the humbleness of the servant's calling is not one of them. When men come to possess this power, whether by the consent of the governed or not, they become royalty, and royalty demands certain prerogatives. Chief among these are obedience, praise, and pomp. Their ears are tickled by flattery; they are guarded from everything which is offensive or dangerous; they do not share the arduous life of the citizens. They live on a plane above their subjects; luxury is regarded as their desert.

This assumption of royalty is accepted by the subjects of kings, and they even rejoice in it, for a state takes on distinction and an appearance of power through the spectacle of the pomp and glory of its ruler. The king does not serve—he is served. His authority is built up and maintained by the obedience of the masses. No nation can afford the spectacle of shabbiness on the part of its ruler. The function of leadership is necessary for the welfare of the state, but the efficiency of that leadership is impaired to the extent that the ruler is pampered, measuring greatness in terms of authority. Jesus saw this as the pattern of the political when he said, "The kings of the Gentiles exercise lordship over them . . ." (Luke 22:25).

Though the Jews set themselves apart from the Gentiles, they were not able to free themselves from the thinking of their neighbors. They thought of their nation as a theocracy and spoke of the coming kingdom of God. They insisted that their highest interest was in religion, in keeping the Law of their God. But in their behavior and thinking about their political fortunes they did not differ widely from the nations around them. There was the same spirit of nationalism which seems to afflict all nations, the belief that one's own group is called by God to rule over others because of the superior quality of its culture. Though this desire to impose their blessings upon their neighbors is made to appear altruistic, at its heart it is selfish. It may be promoted with high-sounding shibboleths—to promote freedom and the like around the world—but at the core there is the selfish desire to be looked up to and to rule. Judaism of Jesus' day was cursed by a rabid nationalism. The Jews believed it was the will and purpose of God that they should rival their neighbors or even rule over them.

A word may be said about the rise of the term *kingdom of God.* Though the exact phrase does not appear in the Old Testament, the idea is implicit in the history and thinking of the Hebrew people. God's promise to Abraham, according to their thought, had been realized in part in their possession of Canaan. When they thought of the future for his covenant people they naturally thought in terms of a political state, calling it the kingdom of God. This idea was promoted in the rise of the apocalyptic literature, of which the Book of Daniel was the first. Here the claim was made that "his dominion is an everlasting dominion . . ." (7:14; see also 4:34; 6:26; 7:27). In the great vision of chapter seven, the Gentile nations are represented by terrible and grotesque beasts of prey. But in the great day of judgment these kingdoms are set aside and a new kingdom, not of evil but of God, is firmly established. It is out of class with those evil kingdoms and is represented by "one like a son of man" (7:13). And the fiat of God went forth and "the saints received the kingdom" (7:22).

Another form of expectation was that represented by the Son-of-David motif. It traced back to the early references to a Messiah who would come from the Davidic line. (See Isaiah 9 and 11.) Out of a line of Davidic kings would arise one who would be above all who had gone before, and who would be in the favor of God in unique fashion. This older idea of a Messiah was represented in Jesus' day by the Zealot movement. These ardent patriots may have fallen short of an intelligent knowledge of God's will for his people, but they were long on courage and daring, believing that with the help of God they could defeat the legions of Rome. Their plottings finally culminated in the great Jewish war of 66-70 A. D., which ended in the destruction of the Jewish state and the loss of the temple.

A revolutionary spirit had seized many of the Jews, fostered by their extreme nationalism. They believed ardently that it was not God's will that his people should be ground under the heel of the Gentiles, whom they regarded as agents of demonic powers. The Day of Jehovah, which would bring victory, was not far distant. Whether the nationalists would take up arms with the Zealots or wait for Jehovah to intervene with heavenly powers, the hopes of the nation were fixed on that coming day when their political salvation would be assured.

There was another vision, so obscure that it was seen only by those who looked deeper than the surface. It traced back through the centuries and was rooted in the broad vision of the prophets. It was represented in Jesus' day by a group often referred to as *the poor*. The term had come to be synonymous with *the pious*. Among them were men like Joseph of Arimathea, who "was . . . looking for the kingdom of God" (Mark 15:43), and Simeon, who was "looking for the consolation of Israel" (Luke 2:25). They were concerned for God's glory, not for the political supremacy of the Jews; for righteousness rather than for bread and ease. They were indifferent to the fact that the Jews were subject to Rome. That was no barrier to their approach to God.

This thread in the fabric of Jewish culture was a golden one, though hidden. It was a rivulet of sparkling water which found its source in the spiritual treasure of Jeremiah's new covenant and of the Servant songs of Isaiah. Each of these prophets had a vision of things more permanent than national glory, of a spiritual Kingdom in which God would rule in the hearts of his people. They wrote in troublesome times, when the Hebrew nation was breaking up, their cities were being burned, their temple was in ruins, and they were led into captivity to the East.

Surely this was the end of the road for the covenant people. But the writer of the Servant songs begins with
"Comfort, comfort, my people,
says your God" (40:1).

God's purposes for his people have not failed. Ultimately they will triumph.

"I will give you as a light to the nations,
that my salvation may reach to the end of the earth" (49:6).

But it was to be no mere political or military victory. Israel was to triumph by becoming a servant, not a monarch. Israel's weapons would not be carnal weapons, but love and service and, if need be, innocent suffering even to death.

It was this vision of the prophet which captured Jesus. Standing on a high mountain, he saw not empires with marching armies, but the Kingdom of God in its true glory. He glimpsed a new power, not of the material but of the spiritual. He saw a vision of a new earth in which love and patience and service would be the ruling principle. It had not been easy to go contrary to the popular expectation of his day. He had an undying affection for his people and was not unmoved by their sad lot. They were indeed as sheep without a shepherd. He was concerned for their highest interests, that they fulfill their destiny as a covenant people. But nationalism would not accomplish this; it would be their destruction.

What was this Kingdom which Jesus preached so passionately? It had none of the marks of an earthly kingdom, but it was the only true kingdom, for it was the

Kingdom of God. To the Jews it must have appeared as utter foolishness, but their misunderstanding was due to faulty human knowledge. The best of men are prone to set the pattern for God in the mistaken belief that they are promoting his cause. Peter presumed to correct Jesus saying, "God forbid, Lord! This shall never happen to you" (Matthew 16:22). The pattern of the Kingdom which Jesus set was God's pattern; it was the true fulfillment of God's redemptive purpose.

For contrary to human opinion, however high, God's purpose does not consist in a larger and more powerful political state for his people. The human mind seems unable to understand the mind of God. We fail to learn the lessons which human history teaches—that size and numbers and material might do not make for permanence or advance. Great empires rise and then fall, and that from lack of strength from within. And there is no reason to hope that our present empires will be different.

The Jews to whom Jesus spoke, as well as our generation, needed to learn that God's Kingdom is different, built on different foundations. It is eternal; earthly empires are not. The Kingdom of the Servant was not a political kingdom, built and maintained by the means peculiar to institutions of this world. Political power, independence, and patriotism, which are held in high esteem by the world—Jesus had no interest in them. He was not disturbed by the fact that his people were under the iron heel of Rome. His answer to the question, "Is it lawful to pay taxes to Caesar, or not?" (Matthew 22:17), was in essence "It is a matter of indifference." Membership in the

Kingdom is not dependent on political independence or on any other earthly consideration. The pattern of the world has always been that violent force, war, is necessary to protect the nation. But the Kingdom which Jesus was setting up did not depend on armies. "My kingship is not of this world; if my kingship were of this world, my servants would fight . . ." (John 18:36). The spirit of the Servant is not that of violence; however, it is not one of impotence, but truly of power.

The nature of this new Kingdom is in keeping with the character of its founder. If God's Chosen One was to assume the role of a servant, then the Kingdom must agree with this pattern in every particular. All that is contrary to the will of God as revealed in Christ has no place in it. If it differs from worldly empires—and it does—it differs in that it is perfect and they are imperfect or even evil. It is eternal; they are temporary. For that which is imperfect and temporary must give place to the heavenly pattern, in which men serve, not in a slavish spirit under the lash of overlords, but freely out of love and co-operation, in which the only measure of greatness is the measure of service.

Qualifications for citizenship in this Kingdom are in keeping with the character of its Head. Since he adopted the role of the Servant a spirit of service becomes the first requirement for entrance into his Kingdom. "Blessed are the poor in spirit, for theirs is the kingdom of heaven" (Matthew 5:3). It is the meek who shall inherit the earth, even those who are willing to be persecuted for righteousness' sake. In the world children may be highly esteemed but they are never regarded as citizens. They are only potential buyers, potential voters, potential soldiers. But Jesus made strong statements: "Let the children come to me, do not hinder them; for to such belongs the kingdom of God" (Mark 10:14). "Truly, I say to you, unless you turn and become like children, you will never enter the kingdom of heaven" (Matthew 18:3). "The kings of the Gentiles exercise lordship over them; . . . But not so with you . . ." (Luke 22:25, 26).

It is significant that much of his teaching in this strain took place on the last journey to Jerusalem. Strangely blinded, the disciples completely misunderstood the intent of their Master. The road of the Servant was destined to end at a cross, but they persisted in the belief that he would ascend a throne. So, blind to everything but self-interest and pride, they quarreled about chief seats. Jesus made one final appeal to them to show them the true nature of the kingdom. He put on the garment of a slave and washed the disciples' feet. It was not a mere gesture; it was an acted parable, teaching once again that the way into the favor of God was through service, not ruling. "If you know these things, blessed are you if you do them" (John 13:17). This story is the classic on service in all literature. How tragic that his followers after the centuries which have passed have still the same difficulty to understand the mind of the Master!

The Kingdom of the Servant does not depend on material resources. Here again it differs from the political state, the safety of which depends largely upon resources of wealth and of man power. Material security is something much sought for in our day. We have developed skills and harnessed forces beyond the wildest dreams of our fathers, but the unrest and the social ferment have robbed us of peace and assurance of well-being. But Jesus was strangely indifferent to these things. Surely he was touched by the miseries of his world, the hunger of little children, the cries of the helpless. But he had a vision of a world in which man would not prey on his fellows, in which men would seek first God's Kingdom and his righteousness and all these things would then be theirs as well (Matthew 6:33). If the Kingdom came into the world, then the physical needs of men would be supplied in proper measure. But, for him, the material is secondary; the things of the spirit are of first importance. He warned that "unless one is born anew, he cannot see the kingdom of God" (John 3:3).

In the John gospel the distinction between flesh and spirit is pointed up. (See 6:33.) In the synoptic gospels, this teaching is found in Jesus' warning about the dangers of wealth. Mammon becomes the god whom men worship; wealth is the treasure upon which men depend for their well-being. This is the most difficult of Jesus' teachings. He asserted that "it is easier for a camel to go through the eye of a needle than for a rich man to enter the kingdom of God" (Matthew 19:24). Only the Servant, he who was concerned about the highest interests of men, could have spoken in this fashion. Had he made himself an earthly king, he would not have been indifferent to the wealth and the power which earthly kingship brings to men.

The Servant's Kingdom is one of social righteousness. "Unless your righteousness exceeds that of the scribes and Pharisees, you will never enter the kingdom of heaven" (Matthew 5:20). The Kingdom of Christ is not an aggregation of individuals isolated one from another; it is a community in which men love and serve their fellows. It is not enough to abstain from acts of aggression; the motives and desires of the heart must be kept in stern control.

The law of service demands love, and love is based on appreciation. Where no value is allowed, contempt and hatred follow. But love follows naturally when value is placed upon an object. The Jews were commanded to love their fellow Jews, but they felt free to hate their enemies. This is ever the way of the world. Man in his blindness makes imaginary distinctions. The empires of this world have always divided men into two categories, citizens and aliens, and often aliens are divided into mere strangers and active enemies. Nations profess to wage war in defense against aggression by enemies. But Christ allows no such distinctions. He alone saw men as God sees them, all alike in value in his sight. He who alone was able to make distinctions made none. He made no unreasonable requirement when he commanded, "Love your enemies" (Matthew 5:44). The men of the Kingdom must catch this vision of Christ's redeeming love for men; then love for enemies will not be impossible. If men are to be rated as sons of the Father, they must be able to love and serve their fellow men regardless of their social state. For God "makes his sun rise on the evil and on the good, and sends rain on the just and on the unjust. . . . You, therefore, must be perfect, as your heavenly Father is perfect" (Matthew 5:45, 48).

The Kingdom is like Christ the Servant. It has none of the trappings so constantly associated with royalty. Its power is not outward, but works silently from within, transforming the life of individuals and of society. "The kingdom of God is as if a man should scatter seed upon the ground . . . and the seed should sprout and grow, he knows not how" (Mark 4:26, 27). The Servant shall not strive or cry aloud, but he is not weak or ignoble. His is the true dignity of one who became a savior—not the tawdry glory of an earthly ruler who must bolster his fame by his power over the bodies of men. The dignity of Christ is measured by the true worth of a matchless character and by the importance of the work he came to accomplish—the salvation of men. His glory is an imperishable glory. There have been great empires, as measured by the yardstick of the world, and those who sat on the thrones were given honor and even divine worship. But empires have continued to fall and their kings are forgotten. But he who made himself of no reputation, becoming a servant, has established a Kingdom which will not crumble into dust, because it is builded on the sure foundation of the love and power of God. The Kingdom of the Servant is the Kingdom of God.

CHAPTER TWELVE

The Servant's Last Journey

He set his face to go to Jerusalem (Luke 9:51).

That last journey to Jerusalem, which brought Jesus to a Roman cross, was marked by deep gloom; he indeed walked through "the valley of the shadow of death." He was absorbed in the thought of the threatened danger of this new venture. Everything seemed to conspire to make this the most tragic chapter of his life thus far. The shadow of the cross fell athwart his path and cast its gloom upon his countenance. The days and months of his ministry which had passed had not been seasons of unalloyed gladness and light; he who had accepted the role of the Servant could never be carefree. Jesus was by no means gloomy. Rather, he was by nature cheerful and composed, because he was always aware of God's presence and favor. In his companionship men found assurance and strength. He was confident that he knew the mind of God and that he held in his hands the secret of power which could free men from their shackles of sin.

But he could never give himself to unrestrained gaiety—he was the Servant of Jehovah. The woes of men and women and little children weighed heavily upon him. Compassion, not complacency, was his constant mood as he looked upon humanity. His people were as "sheep without a shepherd." He was moved to righteous indignation against the political and religious systems of his day which bound burdens, hard to bear, and laid them on men's shoulders (Matthew 23:4). The spectacle of Jesus of Nazareth passing by is that of one whose discerning eye saw the burdens and sorrows of his people, and whose heart of pity embraced them all. He saw the poverty and distress of the common people, borne down by the exactions of the rich. He saw the religious leaders who set themselves as shepherds over the people but did not feed the sheep; they were pitiable slaves of their narrow systems, plagued by the sins of the spirit. He saw God's chosen people in the grip of a rabid nationalism which would bring about the destruction of the nation. Truly, in him were fulfilled the words of the prophet:

"Surely he has borne our griefs
and carried our sorrows" (Isaiah 53:4).

The early ministry in Galilee had not been a joyous round of feasts and merrymaking, but a purposeful giving of himself to the redemptive work of God. He had driven himself, often denying himself needed rest and sleep because of the greatness of the task and the urgency of haste; the allotted time was all too short. He must cast out demons and perform cures today and tomorrow, but the third day brought the end of the road. There had been many disappointments. The people ate their fill of the loaves but saw no signs. They came seeking physical cures but very often were unconcerned about their spiritual ills. His constant sorrow was that they were rejecting the good news of the Kingdom. "How often would I have gathered your children together as a hen gathers her brood under her wings, and you would not" (Luke 13:34). Capernaum! Chorazin! Bethsaida! More tolerable for Sodom in the day of judgment than for his people! He had lived and walked and worked among them, but their response had been discouragingly slow. The words of woe he spoke came from a breaking heart, not in anger or gloating over their fate.

All this had taken its toll of strength. He could not lightly wash his hands of those who ignored his offer of salvation and in a spiteful spirit opposed him. But now the gloom had deepened; defeat stared him in the face, and with it disgrace and death. It did not come to him as a surprise. His hour was drawing near. The age-old conflict between good and evil was about to be resolved, and the first victory would go to the enemy. But ultimately in spite of the cross—instead, because of it and through it—victory would come to his cause. It meant grief to our Lord, not for his own fortunes but for those of his people, who were rejecting the offered salvation and would pay a terrible price. It was not, therefore, despair for God's cause which cast its pall of darkness upon this fateful journey. It was rather the gravity of the undertaking, to blaze a new path so strange and contradictory that few would find it at once, that deepened the lines of sorrow on Jesus' face. He had come to cast fire on the earth, the fire of judgment, and he was torn between the desire to delay it and the imperative to carry it through.

He had not been free from danger in Galilee. Herod, with a bad conscience over killing one prophet, was filled with superstitious fear at the news of another. His friends were mocking him, saying that it was John the Baptizer, who had risen from the dead. Herod was curious to see this wonder-worker. He wanted to make sure that the report was not true. Jesus knew well that the curiosity of a Herod was a dangerous thing; the Herods were notoriously jealous of their political fortunes. In this, Antipas was the true son of his father, who had wantonly slaughtered the babies in Bethlehem. Luke 13:31-33 preserves another tradition, which marked Antipas as more than curious. Jesus was advised by friendly Pharisees that Herod wanted to kill him. Jesus had taken the warning seriously and left Herod's territory, spending some time in Phoenicia and Decapolis. Then, turning south from Caesarea Philippi, he had passed through Galilee secretly on his way to Jerusalem.

This visit would be different from earlier visits. Though the Markan tradition gives no hint of any visit to the capital city during his earlier ministry, there are southern sources preserved in both Luke and John which indicate a rather large activity in Judea and Samaria. The occasions for earlier visits were probably the great festivals which would draw Jesus as a devout Jew to the temple. John tells of Jesus' presence at Passover (2:13 ff.), Tabernacles (7:2 ff.), and Dedication (10:22 ff.). But on these occasions his role was probably, in part, that of a worshiper. Now he was going to Jerusalem to press his claims as the Anointed One, and such a course would be fraught with great danger to himself.

This was to be no leisurely trip, turning aside to visit some out-of-the-way village or tarrying with friends. He was in haste. Luke tells us that "he set his face to go to Jerusalem" (9:51). He had always appeared to be under the compulsion of haste. His words, " . . . for that is why I came out" (Mark 1:38), express something of the urgency of his mission. He had limited his ministry to the lost sheep of the house of Israel, not because he shared the common prejudice against the Gentiles but because the time was too short for a wider mission. But now the compulsion seemed even greater; he was moving toward the culmination of his life's work. He was carrying his gospel to the leaders in Jerusalem. Perhaps they might respond, but more likely they would reject him. Something of the gravity of the situation was written on his face, bringing awe and wonder to those around him. In the early days of his ministry in Galilee the people had continually crowded around him, careless if they rudely touched him. On one occasion there had been opportunity for a sick woman to try to secure healing without his knowledge. Now the situation was strangely different. Mark describes it in this fashion: "And they were on the road, going up to Jerusalem, and Jesus was walking ahead of them; and they were amazed, and those who followed were afraid" (10:32). Many of his disciples were expecting some great thing to happen in Jerusalem, but the stern look on Jesus' face coupled with his words of foreboding of evil dampened their enthusiasm. In secret the Twelve quarreled about chief seats, but in Jesus' presence they had grace enough to be ashamed. And the careless crowd sensed a difference in the mien of the Teacher and shrank back in fear.

The behavior of the disciples is difficult to understand.

They seemed to be entirely out of sympathy with their Master. Not long before this they had confessed their faith in him as Messiah, and this in spite of the fact that his conduct had not been in line with popular expectation. It had been indeed the prompting of the Father, rather than human reason, which had inspired their confession. This faith had been of slow growth, yet there had been confidence and understanding with their Master. But now that earlier harmony seemed to have been lost. Jesus had not changed; the role he had adopted in the beginning had not been left behind. Suddenly they gave themselves to vain speculations. They could not dissociate themselves from the nationalistic hopes of their day. Jesus had never by word or deed given any encouragement to this idea; rather, he had made it clear that he had no interest in or sympathy for the Jews' dream of political power.

But the disciples chose to draw wrong conclusions from the importance which Jesus placed on this new venture. Contrary to all that he had said, contrary to the pattern of his life, they apparently expected him to throw off the role of meekness, arrogate to himself authority as a political and military Messiah, and seat himself upon the throne of David. He would marshal an army and with the help of the God of Israel conquer Rome, so they reasoned. In this event there would be chief seats for his friends after the pattern of Oriental royalty. This was heartbreaking to Jesus; it grieved him that they should so utterly misunderstand the true spirit which was in him, and fail to catch his vision of the Kingdom and its Messiah set by the pattern of the Servant. It is significant that the quarrels about greatness, which form such a large chapter of the gospel story, all took place on this fateful journey. Only their misguided belief that God was about to intervene in human history with weapons of violence and death could have led them to behave in such an ungrateful and selfish spirit.

The first occasion is recorded in Mark 9:33-37. As they journeyed, they fell to quarreling; tempers were on edge and voices were raised. They had fallen behind Jesus in the way, but at the lodging place Jesus inquired the reason for their disputing. They were embarrassed and remained silent. But Jesus knew the dispute had been about "who is the greatest in the kingdom of heaven" (Matthew 18:1). Such behavior on their part was tragic. How could they have so completely misunderstood him? But they were possessed by a spirit which was characteristic of their times, a spirit which unfortunately has not been limited to the ancient world but is present in power today.

Dr. Theodore Robinson asserts that personal standing and authority claim greater respect than law and principle do, and that the great person is the one who receives honor, obedience, and service from all who are around him.[1] Jesus took a little child in his arms, embracing it, and declared that unless his followers gave up their ambitious desires and became as little children they could not even get into the Kingdom, much less be great. Then on a later occasion the two sons of Zebedee presumed on their intimacy with the Master and on the influence of their

---

[1] Theodore H. Robinson, *Gospel of Matthew: The Moffat New Testament Commentary,* Doran and Company, Inc., 1928.

mother, who was one of the women who gave of her means for the support of the mission. These ambitious men wanted nothing less than the best seats in the political kingdom which they expected was about to be set up, assuming that Jesus, like an Oriental monarch, would honor his friends by granting them places of honor next to the throne. There is a note of sadness in Jesus' response; they were asking for more than they knew. It would not be the cup of glory, but the cup of suffering and shame, that they would share. Jesus was going to a cross, not a throne. They might well be called upon to suffer martyrdom with him.

In his account of the Last Supper, Luke pictures the disciples quarreling the old quarrel. Who is greatest? And in the John gospel we have perhaps another account of the same incident, when Jesus, in order to rebuke their false pride and teach them the grace of humility, girded himself with a servant's apron and stooped to wash their feet.

It was under such circumstances that Jesus made this fateful last journey to Jerusalem. He was going to challenge the leaders with his gospel of love and present himself as their Savior. He had not abandoned the role of the Servant. He had tested it again and again, and had been reassured by the heavenly visitors on the Mount of Transfiguration. The present perils could not shake his faith and his determination to carry on, though now the hazards against him were increased. Jesus was not an impractical dreamer, as is declared by critics of Christianity or even by some hard-headed Christians who would be realistic; he was the greatest realist of all time. If his nation was to be saved, it would not be through the agencies of nationalism, but by the way of love and service and innocent suffering. His nation was not in any mood to listen to this voice from Nazareth, even as their fathers had not heeded the prophets. But the seed of this new gospel would fall into the responsive hearts of those who were hungering and thirsting after righteousness, and would bring forth a harvest unto eternal life.

But the leaders of the covenant people of God would be deaf to the Word of God. They were held in the grip of nationalism, a pattern of the world and not of God. It was the Roman pattern; empires are created and maintained by violent force. The *Pax Romana* was the peace imposed by the Roman legions. It is still the pattern of the world. The citizen of a modern imperialistic nation is easily persuaded that military victory is necessary for the welfare of its citizens; so, war is justified and even glorified. But Jesus turned this pattern upside down. "But not so with you; rather let the greatest among you become as the youngest, and the leader as one who serves. For which is the greater, one who sits at table, or one who serves? Is it not the one who sits at table? But I am among you as one who serves" (Luke 22:26, 27).

Thus our Lord made that fateful journey to Jerusalem, where the prophets had died. Though he went among the Passover crowds, he walked alone. Not even the Twelve shared his thought and gave sympathetic understanding. There would be a brief flare of hosannahs when he rode into the city, but the crowd would be strangely blind to the fact that their King was in tears. His forebodings of danger would be realized. Creating an uproar, and interfering with the lawful business of the priests would not go unnoticed by either the hierarchy or the Roman governor. Events would move in quick succession; he would presently find himself in the hands of the Romans, and they would crucify him. How terrible to contemplate that God's Chosen One should come to such an end! And yet it was fitting. The cross was reserved for slaves. It was not out of keeping that he who was the greatest Servant of all should be sold by one of his disciples for the price of a slave and should die the death of a slave. He accepted the cross as the "death he was to die" (John 12:33), for by the lifting up on the cross the Son of man would cast out the ruler of this world and would draw all men unto himself.

And in the days to come, his disciples and his church would learn the mystery of the cross and the Servant who died on it. No longer blind to its meaning, they would go everywhere preaching the gospel and turning the world upside down. No longer unwilling and fearful, they too would accept the cross of shame and suffering, "rejoicing that they were counted worthy to suffer dishonor for the name" (Acts 5:41).

CHAPTER THIRTEEN

The End of the Road

"Shall I not drink the cup which the Father has given me?" (John 18: 11).

He had staked all on that fateful journey to Jerusalem—and had lost. The forces arrayed against him had been too strong. He had brought to the capital city his gospel of the Kingdom, God's redemptive purposes for his covenant people, whom we would have saved from a fatal war with Rome.

But in vain. The Great Sanhedrin was entrenched in privilege and authority granted by Rome. This power they were using for their own advantage, not for the advantage of their people. They were in no mood to heed the prophet from Galilee and change their ways; they resented his coming as an intrusion into their rights. When he drove the traders from the temple he sealed his fate. The great outer court they had turned into a bazaar, where foreign money was changed and sacrificial animals and birds were sold. Though Gentiles could not enter the Jewish courts, they were allowed in this outer court and many pious God-fearers came here to worship the God of the Jews. The family of the high priest, though professing to be friendly to non-Jews, cared less for the religious interests of their neighbors than for their own nefarious traffic. All this was out of harmony with the spirit of the great Passover festival.

Pious Jews who made the weary journey over sandy deserts or more dangerous seas, the Diaspora or scattered ones from every nation under the heavens, or those from near-by Galilee and the hinterland of Judea—all these came with singing on their lips, watching eagerly for the first glimpse of the holy city.

"I was glad when they said to me,
'Let us go to the house of the Lord!'

. . . .

Pray for the peace of Jerusalem!" (Psalm 122: 1, 6).

But Caiaphas and his crowd cared little for such sentiments except as they could be converted into selfish profits and political power. Though professing to be religious, they wanted no new brand of religion. Prophets were no more welcome in Jerusalem than Amos had been in ancient Bethel. If they allowed the Galilean prophet free hand, he might stir up a revolt; the volatile, hot-headed Zealots were only waiting for a leader. Every sincere Jew must have been stirred to indignation at the callous indifference to spiritual values on the part of the temple authorities.

There was a sinister tie-up between the political and the ecclesiastical. The high priestly family controlled the Sanhedrin. The prophet from Galilee by his courageous invasion of the temple and his challenge to its leaders might easily have created an uproar of religious frenzy and open criticism, and the leaders would thereby have lost face. Further, they feared that Rome might intervene in case of a disturbance and take away from the Sanhedrin the political power which they cherished so highly. The hard-headed businessman, Caiaphas, could well exclaim, "You know nothing at all; you do not understand that it is expedient for you that one man should die for the people, and that the whole nation should not perish" (John 11: 49, 50). Here was speaking the true politician, hiding his bloodthirsty plans under a pious shibboleth. Unwittingly he was speaking a prophecy of God's gracious gift of salvation through the cross. But do not give him the credit; he was no consecrated mouthpiece of God.

Rome had been on the alert also. The governor of the province was held responsible for safeguarding the interests of the empire. He had an army at his command, placed in strategic spots. One of these garrisons was in Jerusalem, quartered in the castle of Antonia. At feast time special precautions were taken to preserve the peace; the governor would then leave Caesarea and journey to Jerusalem. Rome was ruthlessly efficient. There was no thought of leniency; even free speech was silenced. Perhaps it was only hot words which brought swift death to those "Galileans whose blood Pilate had mingled with their sacrifices" (Luke 13:1). Perhaps the high priest had already informed Pilate concerning the Galilean pretender. The John gospel related that "the band of soldiers and their captain and the officers of the Jews seized Jesus . . ." (18:12). It is probable that all the gospels are inclined to excuse Pilate and blame the Jews instead. Certainly Jesus knew the ruthlessness of a military government well enough to be aware of the danger from this quarter.

Jesus had failed to win his nation. He had done his best; he had carried his gospel to the capital city, but the holy city which contained the Father's house had rejected him and forces were already in motion which would bring him to an ignominious death. He could no longer rely on the crowds to protect him. They were fickle in their loyalty and the leaders had ways of circumventing the crowds. They would seize Jesus by night when the crowds were absent.

His disciples had blindly held on to the hope of an earthly kingdom which Jesus would by some means set up. Now in the shadow of the olive trees they were seized by a foreboding of disaster. One of them was absent, having left the upper room earlier that night. Jesus knew why he had gone; he knew that Judas, his hopes of rewards and favors gone, had in an hour of disappointment and resentment attempted to salvage something from the wreckage, and to revenge himself upon the one whom he blamed for the disaster.

The hour in the garden found Jesus distraught. Again the old doubts assailed him: Had he been following the right course, which had now brought him to defeat? Had it been truly the will of God that he assume the role of the Servant? The road which he had traveled was now ending in a cross. There was another choice he might still make—run away in the darkness and escape his foes. There were hills and caves where he might hide. There were surely friends who would help him escape. But he could not do that. He must follow the Father's will, and the hour in the garden reassured him that he had not mistaken that will. He must face the consequences of this decision, and he knew well what they were. He would be hunted down as a criminal by the Jews aided by the Roman police, and, after a mockery of a trial, would be turned over to the Romans. The dreadful Roman cross would be his fate. Though the struggle in the garden had been intense, so intense that his perspiration flowed like blood from a wound, he was now calm. He had not been mistaken as to God's will; that will had led him to a cross.

It had been a wearisome road which he had traveled. There had been hunger and thirst, labor and fatigue. He had been practically a mendicant, living on charity. There had been no material rewards; he owned no house and land. There had been little honor; the people who accepted him had been for the most part of the lower classes, the *am-haaretz.* The world-minded man shies away from the applause of the rabble; it is a doubtful value. And they had come to him largely for cures and bread, turning deaf ears to his strange preaching about love and brotherhood. They honored the great Hebrew prophets, long dead, but they were no more ready to heed a live prophet than their fathers had been. His disciples could boast of little of worth according to the standards of their day. Some were fishermen, one was a despised tax collector, one was a Zealot, and one was engaged at the very moment in a plot to betray his Master. His disciples were rough and uncouth men, and some of the women of the group were probably not much better. The best known among them, Mary of Magadan, had been a demented woman. His family had brought no honor to the movement; they were embarrassed rather than pleased with him. It had been a wearisome road, and now it was ending in darkness.

It had been a road of failure. As he saw it in retrospect, he had seemed to accomplish very little. The crowds had thronged about him, but only a few could throw off the blindness of their materialism to catch a glimpse of the world of the spirit, to which he would introduce them. They walked in the valleys, not on the heights. Their eyes were fixed on the ground, intent on the muck, not seeing the crown which was offered them. He had not been able to save his nation from an impending war with Rome. Obsessed with their notions of national glory which they expected the Day of Jehovah would bring, they were drifting unheedingly to their fate. The threat of that coming disaster hung like a cloud and made the gloom of the present hour even more dark for Jesus. And he could not forget the cities of Galilee whose judgment he had pronounced with tears, crying, "But it shall be more tolerable in the judgment for Tyre and Sidon than for you" (Luke 10:14).

Even the Twelve, to whom he had given much time and loving attention, had proved a disappointment to him. They had lived with him in intimate fashion, and he had kept back nothing from them. No other mortals ever had such opportunity to know our Lord. They had indeed come to know something of his unique character, even to affirm confidently, "You are the Christ" (Mark 8:29), while the crowds thought him to be only a prophet. But how inadequate had been the faith of the disciples! The

Christ whom they desired was one according to popular fancy—no humble Servant for them! The obsession that he would ascend a throne in Jerusalem had seized them and they had added to his weight of sorrow with their unseemly quarreling over chief seats. The words of the two disciples who traveled to Emmaus on the resurrection day tell of the loss of their high hopes: "But we had hoped that he was the one to redeem Israel" (Luke 24:21). In the garden he had sought strength from the inner circle while he labored in prayer, and they cared too little to stay awake. Within an hour the impulsive Simon, so bold at times, so confident in his allegiance, would play the coward's part and, frightened by a little slave girl, deny with oaths that he had ever known him. And the rest of them would give way in the face of danger and flee in terror, lest they fall into the hands of the soldiers. The cross was too terrible for them to contemplate. Measured according to the standards of the world, his ministry had ended in disappointment and failure.

It had been a lonely road. He had been attended by crowds much of the time since he began his ministry. They had come early in the morning and remained late, roughly thronging him, seeking cures from the wonder-worker and curious to hear what new things he had to say. On one occasion five thousand men had run together to hear him speak. When he rode into Jerusalem they had shouted hosannahs and spread their garments in the dust for him to ride over. In the temple courts they had come to hear him teach, and their presence had been a temporary protection to him.

But few had understood him. His own family had stood aloof, and on one occasion had gone out to seize him because they thought he was demented. Few, even among his closest followers, were able to enter into his thought with intelligent sympathy. And as the days went by they had grown away from him rather than nearer to him. This is described in Mark 10:32: "And they were on the road, going up to Jerusalem, and Jesus was walking ahead of them; and they were amazed, and those who followed were afraid." The time of the old familiarity when they had crowded about him was gone. There was a shadow on his face which puzzled and repelled them. But the fault was not his; it was theirs. Instead of attempting to give sympathetic understanding and comfort in these days of crisis, they in their blindness left him alone. The religious leaders, who should have seen in him the full flowering of the Torah, instead had seen nothing but his cutting across the lines of their pet traditions. He had punctured the bubble of their self-complacency, and they had become vocal in their accusations of blasphemy. With the political leaders in Jerusalem he had never been on terms of politeness. He had never eaten in the houses of the chief priests, as he had done on a few occasions with Pharisees. It had been a lonely road, and it was ending in disaster. In the end, his only companions would be two criminals.

The human in Jesus had revolted at the prospect of the hour, and in agony he had prayed, "My Father, if it be possible, let this cup pass from me" (Matthew 26:39). But he was not overwhelmed at the prospect. He had thrown himself into the arms of God, and he came out of the garden restored in spirit. Convinced again that he had made no mistake, he could say, "Thy will be done." There had come to him the reassurance from God that he was well pleasing to him, just as it had been at the baptism. The role of the Servant had been a humble one, but therein lay its glory. The Servant can be nothing other than humble. The road had seemingly ended in failure, but if it were the will of God, then it could not be failure but success. It had been a lonely road, but he had not been alone at any time; he had had the assurance of the Father's presence and approval, and the sense of that approval would not fade away—the Father would go to the cross with him.

He had set himself to do the will of his Father; that was the passion of his life. Though he had been tempted often to doubt, his knowledge of the truth had driven him to think the program through again, and he had never found that he was mistaken. So though this was the darkest hour of his whole career up to this moment, he was reassured that he had made no mistake—he had done the will of the Father. The role of the Servant was truly the will of God. Therefore he could accept the cup of suffering as approved by God. "Shall I not drink the cup which the Father has given me?" (John 18:11).

But the will of God was not something arbitrary. That may be the proper discipline of the military.

"Theirs not to reason why;
Theirs but to do and die."[1]

God, however, does not rule by arbitrary fiat. Though we

---

[1] From *The Charge of the Light Brigade,* by Tennyson.

may never understand all the mysteries of God's will, yet we are promised light and more unfolding of God's confidence. Jesus was reconciled to the will of God because it was something reasonable. The role of the Servant was in entire harmony with the character and redemptive purposes of God, not one way out of many but the only one which can accomplish salvation for men. The instinct of Jesus, which had led him from the contemplation of grandeur and power and human glory to the humble role of the Servant, had proved to be a true instinct. God's purpose was to redeem mankind, to lift the heavy burdens which crushed them. He was not angry with men; if he had been he would have violently destroyed them. But his entire purpose was redemptive, and the Christ must be a savior, not a destroyer. Only a servant is fitted to lift burdens. Any other role would but add to these burdens.

Jesus had been tempted to become a political Messiah, but he had refused even to use the title; the term carried too great a connotation of human pride and power. Instead he had chosen the humble title *Son of man,* which suggested humility and service. For the political Messiah does not lift burdens, but often creates them. Though he may attempt to conceal his aims under high-sounding phrases and patriotic shibboleths, still the controlling purpose is selfish. He often becomes a victim of a system which fosters human ambition and self-seeking. All his moves are intended in the long run to enhance his glory. Human beings are regimented and used with one controlling purpose—to secure power and fame for himself. The political

Messiah has never lifted the burdens of the world and never will. Men may be better than their systems, but evil systems make even good men their slaves.

Jesus was tempted to become a military Messiah, to use violent force to attain his ends. Does not the end justify the means? The world has continually been fooled by such specious arguments. War has been glorified as the instrument of righteousness: wars to save democracy, wars to establish the four freedoms, even holy wars to defend and preserve Christianity or to wrest the Holy Sepulcher from the infidel. Never was there a more damnable heresy. Nothing has so mocked the cries of the helpless in distress as war. War does not lift burdens, but it lays burdens more ghastly and crushing than does any other agency. Nature in its more violent moods is not the killer that war is. The animals of the forest, with only instinct, are not to be feared as is man, who, when in the grip of this terrible system, destroys his fellow man and himself, both created in the image of deity and endowed with faculties above those of all other creation. War is the great destroyer of property and lives; it degrades and defiles all that is fine and good. It does not feed but brings starvation to the strong as well as to the helpless. War does not bring security, but mocks all hopes for security.

Jesus had been tempted to be a military Messiah, a second Judas Maccabee, a Messiah who would promise to crush the enemies of God and lift up his people. He rejected the temptation. Jesus had been no visionary, no starry-eyed idealist, when he rejected the role of the political and military Messiah. His instinct for truth was right, though he had been compelled to go contrary to the accepted pattern, not only of his time, but of all times. Were he here in person today, he would be faced with the same temptation and would make the same decision.

If burdens are to be lifted, it must be the Servant who will do it. No one else is qualified. If men are to be saved, it must be by a savior, not by an overlord. It is a humiliating role, viewed from the human standpoint. Servants have ever been looked down upon; slaves have ever been despised. There is no honor or dignity in slavery. Suffering and shame and neglect have been the lot of slaves. Death is the only relief, and it may come in violent fashion.

But the earlier vision of Jesus had been vindicated—God would lift the burdens of mankind through him who made himself the greatest servant of all. He who believed that he stood in the position of special favor with God was willing to forego any advantage that might accrue and chose the path of humiliation and service and suffering, a road which would presently end on a cross. He exhibited in his life and ministry what had been in the mind of God from the beginning, a plan so contrary to and yet so far above human wisdom that only men of high vision like the Hebrew prophets had even caught a glimpse of it. The solemn fact is that atonement is not a matter of propitiating an angry God, but rather of bringing the suffering love of a righteous God to touch and heal mankind in its infirmity and need.

CHAPTER FOURTEEN

The Cross of the Servant

The Lord has laid on him the iniquity of us all (Isaiah 53:6).

We stand amazed at the spectacle of the crucifixion, the death of the Nazarene on a Roman cross. Viewed from the human viewpoint, it was the greatest tragedy in history. He who embodied all the graces of God was condemned and put to death as the vilest of men. He who loved men with a love beyond human understanding died as the worst criminal who ever preyed on his fellows. He who gave himself with an abandon of sympathy for mankind died abandoned even by those to whom he had given most. He who made himself Servant of all died alone as though no one remembered what Christ had done for him. Truly this was the supreme tragedy of history. It is only when we see the cross with the perspective of God, as fully as that may be attained, that it takes on more than historical significance—it becomes victory instead of defeat, the supreme act of God in his redemptive purpose. Then only do the clouds of tragedy lift; then only does the cross become the most beautiful and sacred of all symbols.

It did not come to Jesus as a surprise. When he planned that last journey to Jerusalem while yet in the north country he was fully aware of the dangers before him. Ever since he, at the beginning of his ministry, had adopted the role of the Servant, he knew that his path would be one of dishonor and danger. When he started on that fateful journey he knew that his gospel would cut across the traditions of the elders in Jerusalem. The great rabbis would be affronted by the presumption of a Galilean peasant with his theories of what the Kingdom of God must be. He knew that the high priests and the leaders of the Sanhedrin were jealous of their power and prestige and were ever on the alert lest someone rouse the conscience of the nation against their greed and ambition and the hollowness of their pretensions as religious leaders. He knew that Rome was not kind, only tolerant as long as a subject people kept silent in mute submission. Captive people must expect to be exploited, and any cry for justice and freedom, even inarticulate, might be regarded as rebellion, to be suppressed with cruel force. Thus it has ever been.

The Jews were regarded as chattels, regimented in the interests of the empire. Freedom of thought and speech was limited; there could not be room for long for Jesus and his free speech under Rome. Jesus knew that the crowds, the common people, though not prejudiced like their leaders, were fickle and easily swayed. They had crowded about him for cures and would do so again. But they were easily estranged and could easily be persuaded to ask for another "son of the father," Bar Abba, instead of Jesus when the necessity of making the choice was thrust upon them. It is true that this was done largely by the local crowds, but the Galilean crowds, though inclined to loyalty, could do nothing other than keep silent in their helplessness.

Even his disciples, to whom he had given himself freely in confidence and fellowship, were strangely cold. They had followed him through the months of his ministry. They had even confessed their belief that he was the Messiah, but they had failed to understand him. On this fateful journey they had seemed to be held in the grip of a curious obsession—the Messiah must sit upon a throne. Why did Jesus persist in talking about a cross? Luke attempts to excuse them by commenting that "this saying was hid from them, and they did not grasp what was said" (18:34). So bewildered were they that when the hour of Jesus' trial came they ran away in utter defeat.

When he rode into the city in the midst of the cheering crowds, and when, further, he dared to invade the temple, his Father's house, driving out the traders of the high priest, his doom was sealed. The forces of darkness were arrayed against him. It was "their hour and the power of darkness." The cold-blooded high priests and their Sadducean fellow councilmen, the haughty Roman governor, Pontius Pilate, the lecherous Herod from Galilee, all conspired against him. Judas, the man of Kerioth, became the tool of Jesus' enemies, to carry out their nefarious plot before the feast began. Under the cover of darkness they moved, as sons of the darkness, forgetting the dignity of their office, showing no regard for his innocence and worth. Had they been true Jews in whom there was no guile, they might have caught a glimpse of the true identity of the Galilean, but they allowed pride and arrogance to blind them, and they prostituted their high office in order to serve their base desires. Blind leaders, they could not know that this was the hour of God's visitation.

The minions of the high priests, armed with swords and clubs, tracked him to the garden of Gethsemane. From his tryst with the Father he went out to meet them. Identified as the Master through the treacherous kiss of Judas, he was bound and led back to the city of his enemies. The dreadful night wore on. It had begun with the Last Supper in the upper room; now he was a prisoner of the Jews. He was taken first to Annas for examination and then before the council where the great court with indecent haste condemned him to death. Then early in the morning he was dragged before Pilate, who made a show of reluctance, but did not care enough to release an innocent man against the clamor of the Jews. He was mocked and beaten and spit upon, the prey of the temple underlings and the hardened Roman soldiers; even the members of the great court forgot the high dignity of their office and joined in the disgraceful proceedings.

Early in the day the terrible death march along the Via Dolorosa was enacted. He had endured the terrible Roman beating, something so severe that men often died under its lash. And now, his back and shoulders a mangled pulp of bleeding flesh, he went forward under the lash of the soldiers, bearing the badge of his shame and the instrument of his torture, the cross upon which he must die.

The only note of voluntary kindness in the whole procession was the sympathy of certain women of Jerusalem who "bewailed and lamented him" (Luke 23:27). Added to this was the unwitting kindness of Simon of Cyrene, who was impressed by the soldiers to carry the burden under which Jesus had fainted. The crowds followed, some out of morbid curiosity to look upon men dying, some hateful in the cruel satisfaction at the spectacle of another's suffering. Surely there were kindly souls in that tragic procession who remembered the kindness of the Galilean or who, although strangers to him, revolted at the savage cruelty of a Roman execution. But any kindly impulse to protest was suppressed in a feeling of helplessness—it was a field day for the forces of darkness. The gospel record draws a veil of reserve over the horrid event. Mark says simply, "And they crucified him . . ." (15:24). He had been abandoned by the Twelve as early as the arrest. Of his company only the beloved disciple and some faithful women were present when he died.

It was the end of the road; the last act of the drama of the Servant was played on a cross. He could only commend himself into the hands of the Father, and after the hours of agony bow his head and give up his spirit. The eyes which had looked for the last time upon the city and the house of the Father became sightless; the Servant was dead. During these hours, what thoughts had run through his mind? Did a vision of the hidden years come into his mind, of home and mother and the carpenter shop, of the quiet town, of the green hills and the sparkling lakes of Galilee? Was it in the delirium of pain that he cried, "Eli, Eli, lama sabachthani?" (Matthew 27:46), or had doubts assailed him again?

But the torture was finally over for the Nazarene. His feet would never again walk the highways of Galilee.

The hands which he laid in blessing and compassion on the helpless were dead flesh, nailed to the arms of the cross. There was nothing more to do than to take the body down, marred and broken by thorns and thong, by nails and spear, and with unseemly haste commit it to the nearest tomb, lest the city of Annas and Caiaphas be defiled! It was to the credit of two members of the court that they provided a proper tomb for him who in his lifetime had no place to lay his head. Here they buried the body, wrapping it in linen cloths with spices. "Mary Magdalene and Mary the mother of Joses saw where he was laid" (Mark 15:47). And so the sun set on that black Friday. In the city the festival was on—the Passover, which commemorated the Jews' deliverance from the bondage of Egypt. But they had just now killed the one whom God had sent to deliver the nation and all men from the bondage of sin. He was the true Passover Lamb, "who takes away the sin of the world" (John 1:29).

It is vain to presume that we may know fully what was in the mind of Christ as he came to his death, or what was in the mind of God, who sent him to the cross. We are hindered by our humanity from knowing the mind of God fully. And the death of Christ, which is at the center of God's redemptive plan, is in its very nature a mystery. We drop the plummet of our search, but we may never fathom its depths. Sincere minds have since that day searched diligently to find the meaning of the cross, which by a strange contradiction is a symbol of both shame and glory, of weakness and power. Certainly the Jews, who had built up an expectation of a coming Messiah, had not envisioned a Servant Messiah. They expected their deliverer would come as an earthly king and a military conqueror, who would reign on a throne, not hang on a cross. The disciples had been in accord with this view. But it had become increasingly evident that Jesus was not going to fulfill their expectation, and his death finally destroyed their hopes. "We had hoped that he was the one to redeem Israel" (Luke 24:21).

But the resurrection revived their faith in him as the Redeemer of Israel. Gradually they formulated the doctrine of the atonement. Jesus' death could not have been accidental or merely incidental. Hear Peter say on Pentecost: "This Jesus, delivered up according to the definite plan and foreknowledge of God, you crucified and killed by the hands of lawless men" (Acts 2:23). The death of Jesus was according to the plan of God; they found it foretold in the Scriptures. But they did not neglect to blame the Jews for it.

Though we may never fathom all the meaning of the cross, its redemptive aspects shine clear to the believing heart. "God was in Christ [on the cross] reconciling the world unto himself . . ." (2 Corinthians 5:19). But we sense this truth, rather than demonstrate it by dialectic argument. As we stand in awe and bewilderment before the cross, gradually the tangled threads assume an orderly pattern of truth and beauty. Darkness gives place to light. The death of the Sinless One ceases to be tragedy and becomes redemption. The cross is no longer a symbol of shame but of glory; its ugliness becomes beauty, and its weakness strength; the defeat of the cross has become victory. So the cross becomes the most loved of all symbols and the heart cries out, "I believe." Only the hindering veil of our humanity holds us back from a clearer vision.

What are some of the insights which reward our search for the meaning of the cross? The many theories of the atonement are but the results of the search of sincere believers for the truth. No one has all the truth, but every sincere searcher will be rewarded with fresh insights.

There are certain affirmations which may confidently be made. First, in going to the cross Jesus was fully in the will of God; he had consciously followed that will from the beginning, and it led him to the cross. It was humanly possible for him to have evaded the cross at that time. He could have stayed away from Jerusalem, or even at the last moment he could have escaped from the city. Had he ever been tempted to leave his unbelieving people behind and go to the Jews of the Dispersion? But it was the will of the Father that he drink the cup. He could not act apart from the will of God. He went to the cross, confident that God had sent him, and he died with the sense of God's presence. "Father, into thy hands I commit my spirit" (Luke 23:46).

It was not merely a martyr's death; it was that, but more. Precious to the Lord is the death of his saints. The blood of the martyrs is indeed the seed of the church. But he was more than a martyr for he was more than a man. To say that he was the best of men is an understatement. The ultimate meaning of the cross for us rests upon the fact that he was unique, out of class with humanity. To suffer for a good cause is indeed a worthy act, but only the suffering of him who was God incarnate could work complete atonement.

There is a further affirmation: The death was inevitable, but not that he was going to the cross by a fiat of a God who would decree it without reason. It was not inevitable in the sense that it must occur at a given spot at a given moment, or that certain persons must be his executioners. It was inevitable in this, that when the embodiment of the perfect goodness and perfect truth of God met the entrenched sin of the world there was certain to be a cross at this stage of the road. Apparently the first victory in the final conflict between good and evil, between God and Satan, would be won by the powers of darkness. And there would be other crosses to follow, which Jesus' followers must bear, crosses of shame, of scoffing and ill-repute, even of martyrdom.

But we hasten to say that though the death was inevitable it did not mean that his mission had ended in defeat. The Incarnation had not been in vain. The road of the Suffering Servant had not ended in despair. God had turned defeat into victory; ". . . it pleased God through the folly of what we preach to save those who believe" (1 Corinthians 1:21). Christ succeeded not in spite of the cross, but through it. He had succeeded by dying himself, rather than by killing. The weapons of this world are carnal, but the weapons by which Jesus conquered were the spiritual weapons of love and service and suffering.

Let us turn to the insight of Paul. He confidently declared that "God was in Christ reconciling the world unto himself" (2 Corinthians 5:19). This included the cross. Paul declared that the cross "was to show God's righteousness" (Romans 3:25) and that "God shows his love for us in that while we were yet sinners Christ died for us" (Romans 5:8). For Paul, the cross proclaimed God's righteousness. God cannot condone sin, but he does not abandon the sinner. The cross is the supreme expression of God's redemptive love. It is significant that Paul's doctrine of salvation begins at the cross. When Saul, the proud Pharisee, had been shaken from his false security of Jewish legalism his attention was captured by the spectacle of the Crucified One and the cross was transformed from a thing of shame to a symbol of glory.

But how does the cross save men? How can the Christ be the Savior of the world in his role of the humble Servant, which ended on a cross? The answer lies deeper than the so-called moral theory of the atonement, namely, that here the best man who ever lived sealed his faith and loyalty to God on the cross, and that his example should inspire men to the same devotion, that they might earn the favor of God. There are two objections to this theory: first, man is not able to save himself, strive as he may; and second, Christ was more than the best man who ever lived. If man is to be saved, it must be by more than human strength. Only God can save men, and he chose to do it through him who was the God-man. It is true that Christ is our example, but he is the example to men who are already saved; they have been admitted into the favor of God through the cross, and in this new relationship as sons they receive enabling grace to pattern their lives by Christ's.

The secret of the cross lies deeper than man's good intentions. Two basic assumptions are involved. The first is the supreme miracle of all time, the Incarnation. Christ was the Word made flesh, revealing the beauty and reality of God. He was unique with the uniqueness of a perfect life, of a perfect insight into moral and spiritual truth, and of complete authority granted him from God. He was the Anointed One, into whose hands God had given the destiny of mankind.

The second basic assumption is that which appears as the supreme paradox, that God should ordain that this person who was above all men in dignity should assume the role of the Servant. The writer of the Servant section of Isaiah had caught a vision of a new and astounding truth—that the righteous remnant of Israel, suffering innocently for the sins of their leaders, should be able to conquer the Gentiles who had enslaved them, by becoming servants in humility, suffering even unto death; that such servitude and suffering, endured humbly yet with a conviction that it was in the will of God, was redemptive. God would save men, not by slaughtering them but through his people who endured hardship and suffering, loving and serving their enemies, even dying as martyrs. This was the fulfillment when God would send his Anointed One, who was to become the Servant of the Lord.

The innocent suffering of men is vicarious to a degree but not sufficient to accomplish full salvation for others. But the death of Christ was the death of a perfect person, one who was divine, and it saves to the uttermost. For only God can save men, and he did it through the Incarnate

One, who, taking the burden of man's sin on his shoulders, went to the cross. "God was in Christ reconciling the world to himself." Here the suffering love of God came to its full expression.

But this act of atonement does not avail if it is not accepted by the sinner. Paul calls this acceptance faith; faith is the response of sinful man in his need to the grace of God. Man's faith meets God's grace at the cross of Christ. God offers his salvation as a gift to all men, but he does not thrust it on them. Sinful man meets the God of suffering love at the cross of Christ. Here is an exhibition of the righteousness of God. Seeing it, the sinner cries out:

"When I survey the wondrous cross
On which the Prince of Glory died,
My richest gain I count but loss,
And pour contempt on all my pride."

The cross is also the exhibition of the love of God—the love of God for lost sinners. God must be righteousness; he cannot do otherwise than be true to his own character. From the beginning he has been revealing himself to mankind. And this despite the intrusion of sin into the bloodstream of the race. The Bible is the record of God bringing to bear all his spiritual resources to redeem men and bring them back into harmony with himself. It was for this close spiritual union that man was designed. God loves men because of their value in his sight. And this despite man's unworthiness. God's love is intensified by man's lost condition. For the moment the shepherd was more concerned for the lost sheep than for the ninety and nine safe in the fold.

Here then is the conclusion. The death of the Incarnate One, who saw and loved men as only God can and voluntarily took man's burdens of sin upon himself as only the Servant could, was able to make atonement for every sinner who commits himself into the hands of the Savior. Fulfilled is the promise which he made: "Come to me, all who labor and are heavy-laden, and I will give you rest" (Matthew 11:28).

CHAPTER FIFTEEN

The Vindication of the Servant

Therefore God has highly exalted him and bestowed on him the name which is above every name, that at the name of Jesus every knee should bow, in heaven and on earth and under the earth, and every tongue confess that Jesus Christ is Lord, to the glory of God the Father (Philippians 2:9-11).

It was the night following that black Friday. The broken body of the Nazarene had been removed from the cross and hastily laid in a near-by tomb. The apostles were in hiding for fear of the Jews. Only a few loyal women had dared to go to Golgotha, and, waiting only till the Sabbath was over, they would visit the tomb to anoint the body of their Lord with spices. In the city the feast, apparently no different from other Passovers, was in progress. Pilate might have an uneasy conscience for having allowed an innocent man to die on a cross, yet Rome could only commend him for his act—the Nazarene might have been an insurrectionist! The high priests were complacent, because the one who might have aroused the conscience of the nation against their greed for power was safely out of the way. Guarding against a possible plot by the Nazarene's followers to steal the body, they had secured the protection of a Roman guard and the Roman seal.

For those nearest him, all was over. Their hopes for

a kingdom were defeated. "We had hoped . . .," they were saying in sorrow and despair. They must go back to their homes and pick up the threads of their lives which had been broken when they heeded the winsome call of the Nazarene. There would be memories of past days, memories of his gracious presence, of his words and deeds of mercy. Even the tragedy of the present hour could not blot out the poignant memories of those days. But it was only the braver souls—perhaps only the faithful women like Mary of Magadan—who still clung to their faith and hope in a hopeless situation. They were not hiding behind locked doors; at the dawning of that first Lord's Day they would be on their way to the tomb.

But when that day dawned, something had happened. The stone had been rolled from the door of the tomb, and they saw a vision of angels, who declared, "He is not here; for he has risen, as he said" (Matthew 28:6). Helpless were the Roman soldiers; the power of Rome could not prevent the flaunting of the seal of its authority. Two of the disciples going that day to Emmaus were deeply stirred as they walked with a stranger. Their hearts burned as they listened to his words. And then, in the breaking of bread at the inn, the stranger stood revealed as their Lord, living, they knew not how. Mary, weeping at the tomb, mistook Jesus for the gardener, but she forgot all her heartbreak at the familiar word, *Mary*.

The Servant had been forever vindicated. The strange road which he had walked—facing misunderstanding and opposition, regarded at best as a religious fanatic, ending his life on a cross reserved for slaves and criminals—had ended, not in defeat, but in victory. If men had not been blinded by their humanity and their sin, they would have seen from the beginning in the lowly Nazarene the full flowering of God's revelation. Now they must come to terms with the Servant. His humiliation was not weakness. Now it came to be seen in a new perspective; everything, even the cross, had been within the will of God. With a new insight his disciples read the Scriptures anew and discovered what had been hidden under the overlay of Jewish nationalism: how God had long ago pointed out the road which his ongoing Kingdom was to take—the prophet Jeremiah looking to a new covenant, not the superficial one of national ambitions but the reality of the spiritual one; the writer of the Servant section of Isaiah painting that strange but compelling picture of Israel attaining the covenant ends, not in political and military might but by the strange road of love and service and suffering. Here God through his prophet was giving a foreglimpse of his Messianic salvation. Salvation for mankind could come only in this manner. The Coming One, who, not in a servile spirit but with a clear vision of God's purposes, accepted the role of a servant—he alone could lift the burdens of men.

By an unexpected miracle all had been changed for the disciples. How, they did not know. Outwardly, this change had been wrought by the resurrection of the Crucified One, the evidence of which they could not doubt. They had seen the Lord. He had spoken to them and that experience turned their despair into assurance. There could be no going back now. But shall we doubt that there were spiritual forces released by the death and resurrection which would bring to them a world of new insights and powers? Now they realized that the humiliation and shameful death of their Master was not a disaster but that Jesus from the beginning had accepted it as planned for him by the Father. In the light of this new understanding, the faltering Simon, who had denied his Lord in cowardly fashion, became the inspired prophet of Pentecost and the valiant defender of the faith before the Sanhedrin.

And so it was with them all. The nationalistic hopes which characterized Judaism had no longer a place in the thought of the church. There is no record of quarrels over chief seats which had plagued the Twelve before Jesus' death. Instead, they girded themselves with humility to serve one another. The proud Pharisee, Saul of Tarsus, was happy to call himself the slave of Christ. Not ashamed of the gospel of a crucified Lord, he could confidently declare that the cross, which was to Jews a stumbling block and to Gentiles foolishness, was indeed a divine power and a divine wisdom.

The church became indeed the church of the Servant. The proclamation of Jesus, "Blessed are the poor in spirit," was realized in his church. It was true, as Paul pointed out, that the early church was recruited largely from the lower classes; "not many of you were wise according to worldly standards, . . . but God chose what is low and despised in the world, even things that are not, to bring to nothing things that are . . ." (1 Corinthians 1:26, 28). But it was more than an accident of social standing that when, later, men and women of high rank joined with them, the same spirit of humility was maintained. Master and slave sat side by side at the Lord's Supper. The church had caught the true spirit of the Master; humility was not a hardship thrust upon them. Love and service, not the desire to rule, marked the church. Luke was happy to report that "no one said that any of the things which he possessed was his own. . . . There was not a needy person among them . . ." (Acts 4:32, 34). The pagan world was amazed at the new pattern of life of the Christians and often exclaimed, "Behold how these Christians love one another."

It was inevitable that the church would be persecuted. Jesus had predicted it because the world at large was not ready to accept this new experiment. The world no more understood the spirit of the church than had the Jews understood Jesus. But never in those early centuries did the church depart from the pattern set by the Lord. There is no record that the early Christians ever used weapons of violence to defend themselves. So fully had they imbibed the spirit of him who became the Suffering Servant that they prayed for their enemies, rendering good for evil. And the careless crowds who had gone to the arena to gloat over the bloody death of Christian martyrs went away sobered with a strange feeling that these, even in their dying agonies, had conquered. And, indeed, Christianity did conquer and displace paganism, not through political or military force but through the moral compulsion of the church of the Servant.

God had vindicated his Son, whom he sent into the world in the role of a servant. The Roman Empire fell and its emperors are but names on the pages of history. Their pretensions of divinity are remembered only to make them objects of pity or derision. The empire passed, but the church which it had vainly attempted to exterminate lived on. The church persisted because it has its life in him who is eternal. Civilizations may fall and fade away, but Christ continues. His glory does not fade but shines more brightly as time goes on. The Servant has been vindicated. He towers above all men, even the so-called great ones of the earth. For they, as their fathers of old, stand revealed, not in strength but in weakness—victims of ambition to rule, of pride in their earthly estate. They are doomed to be forgotten as were the heroes of old. Men can find permanence only in him who "is the same yesterday and today and for ever" (Hebrews 13:8).